Knowledge and Understanding of the World

Other titles in the Supporting Development in the Early Years Foundation Stage series

Communication, Language and Literacy, Nichola Callander and
Lindy Nahmad-Williams

Creative Development, Ashley Compton, Jane Johnston,
Lindy Nahmad-Williams and Kathleen Taylor

Personal, Social and Emotional Development, Pat Broadhead,
Jane Johnston, Caroline Tobbell and Richard Woolley

Physical Development, Linda Cooper and Jonathan Doherty

Problem Solving, Reasoning and Numeracy, Pat Beckley,
Ashley Compton, Jane Johnston and Harriet Marland

Also available from Continuum

100 Ideas for Teaching Knowledge and Understanding of the World,
Alan Thwaites

Learning Through Play, Jacqueline Duncan and Madelaine Lockwood

Observing Children and Young People, Carole Sharman, Wendy Cross
and Diana Vennis

Teaching 3-8 3rd Edition, Mark O'Hara

Knowledge and Understanding of the World

Linda Cooper, Jane Johnston
Emily Rotchell and
Richard Woolley

Supporting Development in
the Early Years Foundation Stage

continuum

Continuum International Publishing Group

The Tower Building   80 Maiden Lane
11 York Road   Suite 704
London, SE1 7NX   New York, NY 10038

www.continuumbooks.com

Photographs 1.3 and 6.2 used by kind permission of Paul Hopkins
(MMI educational consultancy services, *www.mmiweb.org.uk*).
Photographs 1.2, 4.2 and 5.1 used by kind permission of Emma Jordan
(E-services, *www.emmajordan-eservices.co.uk*).

British Library Cataloguing-in-Publication Data
A catalogue record for this book is available from the British Library.

ISBN: 978-1-4411-5432-3 (hardcover)
       978-1-4411-3762-3 (paperback)

Library of Congress Cataloging-in-Publication Data
Knowledge and understanding of the world / Linda Cooper ... [et al.].
    p. cm. – (Supporting development in the early years foundation stage)
  Includes bibliographical references and index.
  ISBN: 978-1-4411-5432-3 (hardback)
  ISBN: 978-1-4411-3762-3 (pbk.)
  1. Early childhood development. 2. Education, Preschool–Handbooks,
  manuals, etc. 3. Creative ability in children. I. Cooper, Linda. II. Title. III. Series.

  LB1140.K58 2010
  372.21–dc22
                                                            2010002895

Typeset by Newgen Imaging Systems Pvt Ltd, Chennai, India
Printed and bound in Great Britain by the MPG Books Group

Contents

Author Details

The authors of this book are all experienced educationalists with expertise in early years or scientific development or both.

Linda Cooper

Linda Cooper is a Senior Lecturer in Early Childhood Studies at Portsmouth University. Prior to this she was a primary school teacher in West Sussex and a lecturer in higher education working with Initial Teacher Training students. Linda's specialisms are dance, history and ICT. Pursuing her interest as an ICT coordinator, Linda spent time gaining her MSc in Information Systems where she was involved in studying and designing educational applications. She currently has an interest in exploring creative technology for children in the Foundation Stage and Key One. She is also investigating the application of Web 2.0 technology in the classroom. Linda has a longstanding interest in history – she gained her first degree in history and dance in 1993. Her involvement in history has continued throughout her teaching career. She has recently taught and explored the application of history in the classroom with student teachers at Bishop Grosseteste University College Lincoln.

Jane Johnston

Jane Johnston, one of the series editors, is a Reader in Education at Bishop Grosseteste University College Lincoln. She has worked as an early years primary classroom practitioner and in early years and primary education initial training. She has a particular interest in early years scientific development (Emergent Science) and is passionate about supporting early years development through exploration and play. Her many publications reflect this interest and she is the author of many books, articles and chapters on early years and science education, including *Early Explorations in Science* published by the Open University Press and *Early Childhood Studies* published by Pearsons.

Emily Rotchell

Emily Rotchell (nee Richardson) is a Senior Lecturer in Primary Geography Education at Roehampton University. Prior to this Emily worked as a teacher in primary schools for 10 years, including 4 years as the Deputy Head of an Infant School. Emily is a member of the Early Years and Primary Committee of the Geographical Association and has written articles for Primary Geographer Magazine. She is a Chartered Geographer and a Primary Geography Champion (appointed by the Geographical Association) for the Wandsworth and Kingston Region. Emily won a scholarship in a HERODOT competition in 2008 with an essay entitled; Geography in Primary Education – Relevant and Worth Celebrating, Redressing the Balance and Discussing the Issues.

Richard Woolley

Dr Richard Woolley is a Senior Lecturer in Primary Education and Fellow in Learning and Teaching at Bishop Grosseteste University College Lincoln. His interests include Religious Education, Citizenship, PSHE and issues relating to inclusion, diversity and equality in primary education. Richard has taught in primary schools in North Yorkshire, Derbyshire and Nottinghamshire, including time as a deputy head and SENCO. He is a founder member of the Centre for Education for Social Justice.

Series Editors' Preface

Introduction to the series

Before the 10 year strategy (DfES, 2004) and the Childcare Act of 2006, provision for children under 5 years of age was encompassed in a variety of guidance, support and legislation; *Curriculum Guidance for the Foundation Stage* (QCA, 2000), the *Birth to Three Matters* framework (Surestart, 2003), and the *National Standards for Under 8s Daycare and Childminding* (DfES, 2003). This was confusing for many professionals working with young children. The introduction of Early Years Foundation Stage (DCSF, 2008), brought together the main features of each and has provided a structure for the provision of care and education for children from birth to 5 years of age. More importantly it recognized the good practice that existed in each sector of provision and gives a framework or support for further development.

Learning in the Early Years Foundation Stage

The four themes that embody the principles of the Early Years Foundation Stage (EYFS), (DCSF, 2008) succinctly embody the important features of early years provision.

A Unique Child, identifies the importance of child centred provision, recognizing the rapid development in young children and that each child is capable of significant achievements during these years. It is important not to underestimate young children, who may be capable of action, thinking beyond our expectations. It is easy to think that children are too young or not experienced enough to engage in some ideas or activities, but we need to be open-minded as children are very good at exceeding our expectations. Some children may have particular talents, whilst others may be 'all-rounders'. Some children may have particular needs or disabilities. Each child is unique and it is our challenge to ensure that we meet their particular needs, supporting them and challenging them in their development.

Positive Relationships are essential whilst we support and challenge children so that they move from dependence to independence, familiarity to unfamiliarity, learning how to be secure and confident individuals who begin to understand themselves and others. Positive relationships are key to all areas of children's development. Emotional development requires children to have attachments and positive relationships, initially with close family members, but increasingly with secondary carers, peers and other adults. The link between emotional and social development is very strong and positive relationships will also help children to become independent and develop new relationships and begin to see their position and role in society. Positive relationships also support language development, understandings about the world, a range of skills and indeed play a part in all development.

The context in which children develop play a vital part in supporting them in all areas of development. These contexts need to be **Enabling Environments**, or environments that are secure and make children feel confident, that stimulate and motivate children and which support and extend their development and learning. The environment is made up of the physical and the atmospheric. Both need to be warm and secure, so that children feel safe and comfortable and both need to be motivating to encourage children to explore and learn. The environmental atmosphere is also created by the social interactions of all concerned, providing the security that enables a child to move away from the familiar and explore the unfamiliar in a secure and safe way. Indoor environments should provide opportunities for social interaction, language development and creative activities. Outdoor environments may encourage children to develop physically and an interest in the world around them and with opportunities to explore the familiar and unfamiliar world.

Learning and Development indicates the importance of individual children's unique development and learning. As every child is unique, so they have different learning and development needs and will develop in different ways and at different rates. It is important not to assume that all children develop at the same rate. We know that some children begin to walk or talk at a very early age, whilst others take longer, but this does not indicate what they are capable of achieving later in life. Provision for all children needs to be differentiated. In the early years, this is best done by open-ended activities and differentiated interaction and support. Open-ended activities allow children to use and develop from previous experiences and to differentiate for themselves. Support through modelling, questioning and direction can come from experienced peers and adults and will enable the individual child to develop at a rate appropriate for them.

Working within the Early Years Foundation Stage is not without it challenges. Whilst the principles recognize the individual nature of children and their needs, providing this is a different matter. The Early Years Foundation Stage encompasses children in two traditionally distinct phases of development; from birth to 3 years of age and from 3 to 5 years of age. It involves the integration of three overlapping, but traditionally distinct areas of care; social, health and education. Children will have different needs at different ages and in different areas and stages within the EYFS and the challenge is for professionals to meet these diverse needs. It maybe that the norm for children at each age and stage is quite wide and that as many children fall outside of the norm as within it. Care is needed by professionals to ensure that they do not assume that each child is 'normal'.

In order to effectively support children's development in the Early Years Foundation Stage professionals need to have an understanding of child development and share knowledge and understanding in their area of expertise with others whose expertise may lie elsewhere. Professionals from different areas of children's care and provision should work together and learn from each other. Social care, health, educational professionals can all learn from an integrated approach and provide more effective provision as a result. Even within one discipline, professionals can support each other to provide more effective support. Teachers, teaching assistants, special needs coordinators and speech therapists who work in an integrated way can provide better support for individuals. Paediatricians, paediatric nurses, physiotherapist, opticians etc., can support the health care and physical development of children in a holistic way. Early years professionals, behaviour therapists and child psychologists can support the social and emotional development of children. This notion of partnership or teamwork is an important part of integrated working, so that the different types of professionals who work with young children value and respect each other, share knowledge and understanding and always consider the reason for integration; the individual child, who should be at the heart of all we do. Good integrated working does not value one aspect of development above all others or one age of children more than another. It involves different professionals, from early career to those in leadership roles, balancing the different areas of development (health, social, emotional and educational) and ages, ensuring that the key principles of good early years practice are maintained and developed through appropriate interpretation and implementation of the Early Years Foundation Stage.

Another challenge in the Early Years Foundation Stage is to consider the child's holistic progression from birth, through the EYFS to Key Stage 1 and beyond. Working with children in the Early Years Foundation Stage is like being asked to write the next chapter of a book; in order to do this effectively, you need to read the earlier chapters of the book, get to know the main characters and the peripheral characters, understand the plot and where the story is going. However, all the time you are writing you need to be aware that you will not complete the book and that someone else will write the next chapter. If professionals know about individual children, their families, home lives, health and social needs, they will understand problems, issues, developmental needs and be better placed to support the child. If they know where are child will go next, about the differences between the provision in the EYFS and KS1 and even KS2 (remembering the international definition of early childhood is birth to 8 years of age), they can help the child to overcome the difficulties of transition. Transitions occur in all areas of life and at all ages. When we start new jobs, move house, get married, meet new people, go to university, the transition takes some adjustment and involves considerable social and emotional turmoil, even when things go smoothly. As adults we enter these transitions with some knowledge and with a degree of choice, but young children are not as knowledgeable about the transitions that they experience and have less choice in the decisions made about transitions. Babies will not understand that their mother will return soon, small children will not understand that the friends that they made at playgroup are not attending the same nursery or that the routines they have been used to at home and at playgroup have all changed now that they have gone to nursery or started in the foundation unit at school. Professionals working with children, as they move though the many transitions they experience in the first 5 years, need to smooth the pathway for children to ensure that they have smooth and not difficult transitions.

An example of holistic thematic play

Whilst sitting outside a café by the sea in the north of England, the following play was observed. It involved four children representing the whole of early years from about 2 years of age to about 8 years of age; one was about 2 years of age, another about 3 years of age, one about 5 years of age and the fourth about 7 or 8 years of age. The two older children climbed on top of a large wooden seal sculpture and started to imagine that they were riding on top of a swimming seal in the sea. They were soon joined by the 3-year-old child who sat at the foot of the sculpture. 'Don't sit there' said the eldest, 'You are in the sea, you will drown. Climb on the tail, out of the sea'. The two older children helped the 3 year old to climb onto the tail and she and the 5 year old started to slide down the tail and climb up again. Then the children began to imagine that the cars parked nearby were 'whales' and the dogs out with their owners were 'sharks' and as they slid down the tail they squealed that they should 'mind the sharks, they will eat you'. The 5 year old asked what the people sitting outside the café were and the 8 year old said 'I think they can be fishes swimming in the sea'. 'What about the chairs and tables?' asked the 3 year old, to which the older children replied that, 'they can be fishes too'.

At this point, the 2 year old came up to the children and tried to climb up the seal. The three children welcomed her, helped her climb up onto the tail and join them and asked her what her name was. They continued to play and then the mother of the eldest child came to see if the 2 year old was ok and not being squashed in the sliding down the tail. The children did not welcome the interference of an adult and asked her to go away, because 'we are playing, we are playing'. The mother helped the 2 year old to climb down off the seal and the child started to 'swim' on the floor back towards the seal and the other children. The mother said, 'Oh you are getting dirty, get up', but the child kept on 'swimming'. 'Are you being a dog' said the mother 'don't crawl', but the child shook her head and carried on 'swimming' towards the seal, avoiding the fish and sharks!

In this play episode, the children were engaged in holistic play involving aspects of

- Personal, Social and Emotional Development (cooperation);
- Language, Literacy and Communication (communicating with each other and with adults);
- Knowledge and Understanding of the World (applying ideas about animals that live in the sea);
- Creative Development (imaginative play, involving both ludic or fantasy play and epistemic play, or play involving their knowledge).

The adult intervention was, in this case, unhelpful and did not aid the play and illustrates the importance of adults standing back and watching before they interact or intervene.

Supporting development in the Early Years Foundation Stage

This book series consists of six books, one focusing on each of the key areas of the Early Years Foundation Stage and with each book having a chapter for each of the strands that make up that key area of learning. The chapter authors have between them a wealth of expertise in early years provision, as practitioners, educators, policy-makers and authors and are thus well placed to give a comprehensive overview of the sector.

The series aims to look at each of the key areas of the EYFS and support professionals in meeting challenges of implementation and effectively supporting children in their early development. The aim is to do this by helping readers, whether they are trainee, early career or lead professionals:

- to develop deeper understanding of the Early Years Foundation Stage,
- to develop pedagogical skills and professional reflectiveness,
- to develop their personal and professional practice.

Although the series uses the sub-divisions of the key areas of learning and strands within each key area, the authors strongly believe that all areas of learning and development are equally important and inter-connected and that development and learning for children in the early years and beyond is more effective when it is holistic and cross curricular. Throughout the series, links are made between one key area and another and in the introduction to each book specific cross curricular themes and issues are explored. We recognize that language development is a key element in social and emotional development, as well as development in mathematics and knowledge and understanding of the world. We also recognize that the development of attitudes such as curiosity and social skills are key to development in all areas, recognizing the part that motivation and social construction play in learning. In addition, the books use the concept of creativity in its widest sense in all key areas of development and learning and promote play as a key way in which children learn.

Although we believe it is essential that children's learning be viewed holistically, there is also a need for professionals to have a good knowledge of each area of learning and a clear understanding of the development of concepts within each area. It is hoped that each book will provide the professional with appropriate knowledge about the learning area which will then support teaching and learning. For example, if professionals have an understanding of children's developing understanding of cardinal numbers, ordinal numbers, subitizing and numerosity in problem solving, reasoning and numeracy then they will be better equipped to support children's learning with developmentally appropriate activities. Although many professionals have a good understanding of high quality early years practice, their knowledge of specific areas of learning may vary. We all have areas of the curriculum that we particularly enjoy or feel confident in and equally there are areas where we feel we need more support and guidance. This is why each book has been written by specialists in each area of learning, to provide the reader with appropriate knowledge about the subject area itself and suggestions for activities that will support and promote children's learning.

Within each chapter, there is an introduction to the key area, with consideration of the development of children in that key area from birth to 3 years of age; 3 to 5 years of age; into Key Stage 1 (5 to 7 years of age). In this way we consider the holistic development of children, the impact of that development on the key area and the transition from one stage of learning to another in a progressive and 'bottom-up' way. Chapters also contain research evidence and discussions of and reflections on the implications of that research on practice and provision. Boxed features in each chapter contain practical examples of good practice in the key area, together with discussions and reflective tasks for early career professionals and early years leaders/managers, which are designed to help professionals at different stages in their career to continue to develop their professional expertise.

Jane Johnston and Lindy Nahmad-Williams

Books in the series

Broadhead, P., Johnston, J., Tobbell, C. & Woolley, R. (2010) *Personal, Social and Emotional Development.* London: Continuum

Callander, N. & Nahmad-Williams, L. (2010) *Communication, Language and Literacy.* London: Continuum

Beckley, P., Compton, A., Johnston, J. & Marland, H. (2010) *Problem Solving, Reasoning and Numeracy.* London: Continuum

Cooper, L., Johnston, J., Rotchell, E. & Woolley, R. (2010) *Knowledge and Understanding of the World.* London: Continuum

Cooper, L. & Doherty, J., (2010) *Physical Development.* London: Continuum

Compton, A., Johnston, J., Nahmad-Williams, L. & Taylor, K. (2010) *Creative Development.* London: Continuum

References

DCSF (2008) *The Early Years Foundation Stage; Setting the Standard for Learning, Development and Care for Children from Birth to Five; Practice Guidance.* London: DCSF

DfES (2003) *National Standards for Under 8s Daycare and Childminding.* London: DfES

DfES (2004) *Choice for Parents, the Best Start for Children: A Ten Year Strategy for Children.* London: DfES

QCA (2000) *Curriculum Guidance for the Foundation Stage.* London: DFEE

Surestart, (2003) *Birth to Three Matters.* London: DfES

Introduction to Knowledge and Understanding of the World

Knowledge and understanding of the world

Knowledge and Understanding of the World involves children in developing skills, understandings and attitudes about the world in which they live. In this important key area, children explore and learn about science, design and technology, geography, history, information and communication technology (ICT) and citizenship. Through exploring their familiar world and the experiences in their lives, children learn a great deal about the world around them. They can observe similarities and differences between aspects of the natural and man-made world; similarities and differences between animals, plants, technology, locations, ages, cultures, etc. They can move from the familiar experiences in their world to explore the more unfamiliar experiences, such as plants, animals and people in different locations or technology in different eras. They will begin to recognize patterns in the world around them, such as day and night, seasons, growth, life and recognize the changes that occur as things over time. Children can be looking at toys that their parents and grand-parents played with and compare them to the toys that children play with today and be exploring aspects of science (movement and forces), technology (the way toys work), history and ICT (looking at the history of toys that use ICT). In this way knowledge and understanding of the world is an area that is truly cross curricular, but, of course, it goes further than this, as other key areas of the Early Years Foundation Stage are also incorporated in many experiences. As children explore toys they can be sharing their ideas about the similarities and differences, developing vocabulary and language skills involved in *Communication, Language and Literacy* (see Callander and Nahmad-Williams, 2010). They may sort the toys according to shape, colour or type and count the numbers in each group, thus developing aspects of *Problem Solving, Reasoning and Numeracy* (see Beckley et al., 2010). They may share toys and play with each other, developing important skills and attitudes embedded in *Personal, Social and Emotional Development* (see Broadhead et al., 2010), as well as the fine motor skills of *Physical Development* (see Cooper & Doherty, 2010).

Holistic development in knowledge and understanding of the world

Children's development has been described (Johnston, 2005) as like simulta-neously climbing three spiral staircases at the same time; conceptual develop-ment (thinking), skill development (doing) and affective development (feeling). The experiences that children have, either formal or informal, help to support the development in all three areas.

Holistic development of knowledge and understanding of the world differs from this model as the different aspects for the key areas make up the strand for conceptual development; exploration and investigation (science), design-ing and making (design technology), ICT, time (history), place (geography) and communities (citizenship). The development of skills strand may also be divided to accommodate generic skills in all areas, such as observation, interpretation and communication and also specific skills, such as handling variables (science), measuring (science and technology) and mapping skills (geography).

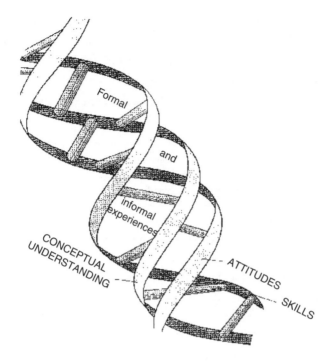

Figure 0.1 The Helix Model of development (Johnston, 2005: 92)

Example of holistic cross-curricular knowledge and understanding of the world

Children can learn in all areas involved in knowledge and understanding of the world through creative cross-curricular play activities. These can also develop other key areas of the Early Years Foundation Stage.

Time travel

In a Foundation Stage unit, the role play area was set up as a Time Machine. Children designed and made space helmets, set up inside of time machine. Children entered the Time Machine by crawling through a tunnel into a corner of the room partitioned off by a bookcase and with a computer to programme the Time Machine. The computer was set up so that children could use it to find routes to different places, search the web to find out about different Time zones and research different eras; for example, their parents' childhood, grandparents' childhood. Inside the time machine photographs of different eras, different locations (town, country, seaside, suburban) and different communities (Hindu, Jewish) were placed on the walls and on a table, toys from different eras were in different boxes.

In one session, five children were playing in the Time Machine and the following interaction took place.

> Josh: *'Where shall we go? I'm the captain'.*
> Martine: *'Let's go to the past. We can be red Indians'.*
> Sean: *'Get your helmets on we are going to take off'.*
> Martine: *'Let's get some stuff first . . . to be Red Indians'* and she and Brittany go to the dressing-up box to get some things to wear. They come back with some material to drape around them to be Red Indians.

Josh pretends to programme the computer and says, *'Get your seat belts on . . . we are taking off'*.

> Brian: *'I am the co-pilot. Let's take off. 10, 9, 8, 7, 6, 5, 4, 3, 2, 1, (the other children join in).*

Brittany and Martine start to squeal.

> Josh: *'We are landing, we are landing'.*
> Martine: *'Are we there/ Where do Red Indian's live?*
> Brian: *'In the past'.*
> Martine: *'They were with the cowboys'.*
> Sean: *'America . . . went there for my holidays'.*

Later, while sitting on the carpet, the teacher showed the children some books about Red Indians and suggested that they find out more about them on the internet. She used the multimedia projector so that all the children could see, and help with, the search and then began to question the children about what clothes the Red Indians wore, when and how they lived. She suggested that the children made themselves a Red Indian headdress using some feathers from the craft area and for the next session there was a table set up with a strip of card, crayons, glue and feathers so the children could make themselves headdresses.

On another occasion one child had visited her grandparents' house by the seaside and she talked about the 'old' things that were there. The teacher used this as stimulus and asked the children to bring in photographs of their grand-parents and parents, so children could look at the differences in clothing, places and photographs. They looked at different toys that their grandparents played with, played with them and made some simple toys, such as spinners. Aabha brought some photographs of her extended family who all lived with her and her grandmother came in to the Foundation Stage Unit to tell the children about her childhood in India.

In this way the children were making their own choices about their learning and developing understandings and skills about the world around them by exploring countries and locations (place), different eras (time), themselves and others (exploring and investigating), technology (designing and making), ICT and traditions (communities). In addition to the learning about the world, the children were exploring in other key areas of the early Years Foundation Stage (DCSF, 2008),

- Personal, social and emotional development; by taking on roles and applying the social rules involved with their play and exploring the social traditions of others (see Broadhead et. al., 2010),
- Communication, Language and Literacy; by communicating with each other in their play (see Callander & Nahmad-Williams, 2010),
- Problem solving, reasoning and numeracy, by counting down for take off (Beckley et. al., 2010),
- Creative development; by using their imagination in their role play, building on their previous knowledge and using it in imaginative contexts (see Compton et. al., 2010),
- Physical development; by crawling into the Time Machine.

Structure of this book

In this book, each chapter is written by an author with experience of teaching and learning in the early years and the specific subject matter. In Chapter 1, *Exploration and Investigation,* Jane Johnston focuses on the specific skills and understandings that make up early scientific development and how these are developed through play and exploration. In Chapter 2, *Designing and Making,* Jane looks at applying specific and general cross-curricular skills to design, make and evaluate a range of technological artefacts and this is a focus also of Chapter 3, *ICT.* In Chapter 3, Linda Cooper discusses the range of information and communication technology (ICT) appropriate for children of this age group and how it can be used to support the development of their skills and understandings about the world around them. Linda is also the author of Chapter 4, *Time* and discusses how young children can learn about time and what historical aspects are appropriate for them to learn about. Chapter 5, *Place*, is written by Emily Rotchell, who has expertise in early years geography development. Time and place are difficult concepts for very young children, who, in their youngest years, have no idea of yesterday, let alone yesteryear. However, Emily discusses what aspects of place are appropriate for children at different stages of the Early Years Foundation Stage. In the final chapter of the book, Chapter 6, *Communities*, Richard Woolley explores how and why children can and should learn about the community they live in and the other communities that make up the world in which they live. Richard draws upon his knowledge in personal, social and emotional development (see Broadhead et al., 2010) and the links between aspects of social development and knowledge of communities and citizenship.

The case studies and reflective tasks will also help professionals to reflect on their own practice, consider the theories and research underpinning effective practice and enable them to identify how they can (and why they should) develop their practice. These case studies are designed at two levels; the early career professional and the early years leader. The early years professional may be a student/ trainee who is developing their expertise in working with young children and, for them, the reflective tasks encourage them to look at the case studies and engage in some critical thinking on issues that are pertinent for early years education. They will also be able to use the chapters to develop their understanding of issues in knowledge and understanding of the world and try out some of the ideas to develop their skills supporting children in this important area of development. The reflective tasks for early career professionals are also relevant to professionals who are in the early part of their career and to help them in their day-to-day interactions with children but also to help them to engage in the national debates about good practice and educational theories. The second level of reflective tasks are geared toward the early years leader, who has a strategic role to develop the practice of those who work with them and also the children in the early years setting. They would be interested on the impact on both the adult professional development but raising standards in knowledge and understanding of the world in young children in their setting. The reflective tasks may well be ones that can be addressed as part of a staff meeting or staff development session and can follow the practical tasks so that professionals at all levels can share ideas and experiences, identify factors affecting their support for children, both positive factors and challenges to overcome. In this way professionals can discuss their own and other's practice, share successes, support each other and come to realize that there is not one model of good practice, one recipe, that if we all follow will automatically lead to success in children's development and help the setting achieve outstanding recognition in inspections.

We hope that professionals reading this book both enjoy and find the content useful in their professional lives.

Summary

The main issues in this book are,

- Knowledge and Understanding of the World involves development in six distinct areas of knowledge; science, design technology, information and communication technology, history, geography and citizenship.
- These six areas are inter-linked and can be developed together and also in activities that span other key areas of the Early Years Foundation Stage.
- Practical involvement, especially exploration and play are ways that children can develop knowledge and understanding of the world.
- The development of generic and specific skills is important in this key area of the Early Years Foundation Stage.
- Experiences in this key area start from the children's familiar world and later begin to explore the less familiar.

References

Beckley, P., Compton, A., Johnston, J. and Marland, H. (2010) *Problem Solving, Reasoning and Numeracy.* London: Continuum

Broadhead, P., Johnston, J., Tobbell, C. and Woolley, R. (2010) *Personal, Social and Emotional Development.* London: Continuum

Callander, N and Nahmad-Williams, L. (2010) *Communication. Language and Literacy.* London: Continuum

Compton, A., Johnston, J., Nahmad-Williams, L and Taylor, K. (2010) *Creative development.* London: Continuum

Cooper, L. and Doherty, J. (2010) *Physical development.* London: Continuum

DCSF (2008) *The Early Years Foundation Stage; Setting the standard for learning, development and care for children from birth to five; Practice Guidance.* London: DCSF

Johnston, J. (2005) *Early Explorations in Science 2nd Edition* Maidenhead: Open University Press

1 Exploration and Investigation

Chapter Outline

Introduction

Finding out about the world you live in involves children of all ages in exploring, discovering and to a lesser extent (but increasing with age) investigating. Exploration involves children in observing the world around them, asking questions about things that intrigue them and following up these questions with further inquiry (Johnston, 2005). Through exploration children develop social and inquiry skills and attitudes which support further learning. They also develop important cognitive understandings which support them through their learning in other areas. Exploration is an important part of the scientific process (Johnston, 2005) and one that can be neglected in busy settings, where professionals are lacking in confidence in the subject matter and where time is limited. The main characteristics of exploration are,

- it is initiated by children's curiosity, or professionals providing motivating experiences;
- it involves children observing, questioning, classifying, hypothesizing and making sense of their world;
- it can lead to planning for further enquiry (exploration or investigation);
- it is collaborative and children can learn as much from each other as from knowledgeable adults, developing language and social skills as well as inquiry skills;
- it can be supported by knowledgeable adults.

Discovery, a popular 1960s and 1970s learning approach (see DES, 1967), has been misinterpreted in more recent times as playing without purpose or objectives and based on the incorrect assumption that children are blank slates as in Locke's (1632–1704) *empiricism*; that is they do not take into account existing conceptual models of the world developed from their previous experience. In reality, it is more akin to exploration and has the following characteristics (Johnston, 2004).

- It is child centered;
- It stems from children's own initial curiosity;
- It involves the construction of understandings, skills and attitudes;
- It is supported and encouraged by adults who ensure that explorations and discoveries are meaningful to the children;
- It involves professionals in utilizing knowledge about the children and learning to provide an excellent learning environment.

Investigations involve more systematic inquiry to answer specific questions. Good investigations stem from explorations and discovery and are ways to answer some questions raised by children. They involve children in planning, predicting, controlling variables, measuring and interpreting. These are higher order skills that develop where children are supported in their explorations. The characteristics of investigations are,

- it involves structured inquiry;
- it can be initiated by the child or professional;
- it will be highly structured to support children in the early years;
- it utilizes higher-order skills which need to be developed prior to use;
- it is more appropriate for children at the end of Key Stage 1 and Key Stage 2.

In this way, investigation is not a term I would advocate in the early years foundation stage, as the approach is more suitable for older children.

The development of exploration and investigation

We know that every child is unique; *'a competent learner . . . resilient, capable, confident and self-assured'* (DCSF, 2008: 5) and in this area, as in any other, children develop cognitively, socially, physically and emotionally in a holistic way. Exploration and investigation involves children developing a range of physical skills, the most important of which is observation. Observation is an essential inquiry skill in the early years (de Bóo, 2004; Johnston, 2005; DCSF, 2008), although there does not appear to be a great deal of understanding about it in young children. In science it is not always seen as the starting point of an exploration (National Research Council of the National Academies, 2007) and it often involves teachers making observations, while children watch (Kallery & Psillos, 2002). Observing an unusual phenomena, having the time to observe or observing familiar events and phenomena in a different way can be extremely motivating, encouraging curiosity and the skill of questioning. I have heard children question why they can see themselves *'the wrong way up in a spoon'*, how manufacturers *'get the drink into a carton'* and why *'shadows go long and thin in the afternoon'*. It can also lead to other important exploratory skills, such as classification; the ability to recognize similarities and differences. Children will naturally sort objects and group things together and classification is an essential element in investigations, where it is necessary to recognize similarities and differences in order to handle variables. They will observe patterns in the world around them; patterns in the daily cycle, seasons, aging and life cycle. They will recognize similarities between natural phenomena, but also the differences; trees all have certain characteristics, but also differences in size, leaf shape, place of growth. They will recognize similarities between houses and localities, but differences between them in terms of the time they were built, the local geography or the climate.

Exploration and investigation will also provide opportunities for children to predict what will happen next; what will happen to puddles on a sunny day, to a planted seed, or to the ingredients of a cake when mixed together or heated. They can also begin to explain why things happen (hypothesize) or interpret their observations. They do this using their previous knowledge and experiences. In this way older children or children who have had particular experiences or interests will have more sophisticated ideas on which to draw when hypothesizing or interpreting. As they develop, children will also have opportunities to measure, moving from comparisons of size, length, mass, etc., to using non-standard measurements, to estimating measurements and recognizing the need for standard measures. They can compare baking ingredients measured and estimated, or standard and non-standard measurements. They can predict how long a mud pie will take to dry up or how much sand it will take to fill up a bucket.

Exploration and investigation from birth to 3 years of age

Children explore and investigate naturally and instinctively from the moment of conception. In the womb, they experience the world around them, hearing, feeling, tasting and moving. They use all their senses to explore and make sense of their immediate environment. From birth, their main needs are for food, warmth and emotional security (see Maslow's hierarchy of needs, 1968), but if these basic needs are met, then children will begin to explore and discover the world around them. They build upon the basic reflexes that they are born with (sucking, grasping, kicking) which are designed to keep them safe (see Johnston and Nahmad-Williams, 2008). They learn that water is hopefully warm when they have a bath and that it can get them wet. They discover that when they kick their arms and legs the water splashes and they receive encouragement from their carers. Their sense of touch is acute and they instinctively move their heads, grasp objects and suck. As their eyes focus, they follow objects with their eyes and reach out for them. They do not have fine motor control, but everything they grasp goes into their mouths and so care needs to be taken to ensure that these objects are safe for them.

In the first few months after birth, carers need to provide stimuli for children during their waking moments. They can listen to sounds in the home and outside while on walks, they can lie on a blanket and kick their limbs and feel the warmth of the sun on their bodies (if the seasons and weather permit). They can feel the wind and rain in their faces while being taken out for walks in their prams or pushchairs. They can play with a range of safe toys which are colourful, make noises and move, including mobiles, rattles, soft toys. As they start to eat solid food, they should have the opportunity to use their fingers to feel the food and later to use a spoon to try and feed themselves. Here they will be exploring the different feel of soft and hard food and discover that hard rusks can become soft when sucked and feel good on the gums as they are teething. Bubble baths can be great fun even at an early age and the children can feel the bubbles, blow them and pop them. As they are being changed and dressed, the carer can talk about the feel of the wipes, cream and let the children feel them with their hands and smell them. They can feel the different materials of their clothes and the tooth of a hair brush. As they get older and have more control over their movements, they can make their own soap lather and brush their own teeth or hair and dry their own arms and legs with a towel.

Once children can move around, they can explore further afield, crawling over carpets and grass, climbing onto settees and beds, choosing their own toys to play with. Much exploration can still take place during normal daily routines, such as bath and meal times, but children can explore capacity, different types of food, cutlery etc. Once the children have ceased to put everything in their mouths, a high chair can be used for finger painting, playdough or other messy activities, without getting the furniture messy. Children under three will very often repeat actions to practice and perfect skills and will spend considerable periods of time in repetitive actions, such as opening a box or posting letters through a letter box or playing with a particular toy. This repetition is the basis of the Montessori method (Montessori, 1912), which builds upon this natural behaviour of the child. Sometimes simple activities, such as pouring water from a teapot into a cup, or matching shapes, or threading beads can be set up for children, although more often the children will decide what activity best suits their needs and should be allowed to follow that activity for as long as they wish. I have seen children spending a whole morning painting the shed in their nursery with water or filling buckets with sand and then tipping them out. These children have decided for themselves, which activities to focus on and for how long and need very little intervention from adults and other children. Other children may need to watch an activity and to do it alongside another child or adult to motivate and support them.

Although children of this age are naturally curious, some will be more curious than others and all will need some form of interaction to enable them to talk about their explorations and discoveries, thus supporting their emotional, language and cognitive development. They can look at the colours in the garden or park and see that while leaves are green and bark may be brown, there can be many different shades. They can learn about colours, shape, pattern, animals and plants, developing their vocabulary. As language develops, so will the children's ability to articulate their curiosity in the form of questions and this curiosity can be used to motivate further exploration. The children can also be encouraged to tell others about their discoveries and new language can be introduced and new ideas and observations explored further.

Photograph 1.1 Exploring the world in the first year

There are some children who may be very reticent about touching things, getting dirty or going far away from their adult carer. These children may have been encouraged by their carer to remain clean or reprimanded about touching things or be displaying 'resistant attachment' (Ainsworth et. al. 1978). Resistant attachment is where the child seeks closeness to the carer and does not explore on their own. It is a type of attachment shown in 10–15% of the US children observed by Ainsworth and her colleagues (1978). These children may need to start exploring with their carer and particular encouragement can be given to explore things on their own.

Case study

A collection of toys were introduced to a baby room for children up to 2 years of age. There were eight children in the room aged between 15 months and 3 years of age. The toys included a spinning top, a rattle, a clatterpillar, a jack-in-the-box, a pull back car and a battery operated hen that dances and sings to the 'Birdie Song'. Adam, who was the youngest in the room at 15 months and had only been in the nursery for a few weeks, became fixated with the hen and spent about 30 minutes dancing and waving his arms with the hen. He did not interact with any of the adult carers or children in the room, but was very motivated by the music and movement of the hen. Helen, who was 21 months old, preferred the jack-in-the-box and sat for a long time turning the handle which made the music start and once 'jack' had popped out, putting him back and starting again. Isaac, who was the eldest child in the room (at 35 months) and about to move to the larger room in the nursery with older children, chose to play with a variety of different toys and to introduce them into imaginative games that he was playing.

Reflection for early career professional

- How do you think the age and experience of the children led them to certain types of toys and activities?
- Why do you think some types of toys are suitable for different ages from birth to 3 years of age?
- How would you interact with the different children in this case study to further their ability to explore and investigate?

Reflection for leader/ manager

- What do you consider to be the advantages and disadvantages of having children from birth to 3 years of age together in the nursery?
- How do the toys you provide encourage exploration and investigation using all the senses?
- How can you support the professionals in your setting to encourage and develop exploration and investigation through everyday experiences?

Exploration and investigation from 3 to 5 years of age

Children between the ages of 3 and 5 years of age are able to explore the wider environment, comparing and contrasting the differences between the country and the town, the street and the garden, the seaside and the woods. They should have opportunities to visit places local to them and further afield. The children should be encouraged to listen to the sounds in the environment, smell the different smells, feel the different objects, look for patterns, shapes and colours. They can even continue their explorations of different localities in their settings, through role play. They can practice gardening and growing things in the nursery garden and a garden centre can be set up to promote knowledge and understanding of the world, counting and language development (see de Bóo, 2004). Potatoes, seeds and seedlings can be planted, dug up and cared for. The seaside can be brought to the nursery through the sandpit, sand trough or by putting sand onto a sheet of plastic, bordered by bricks in a corner of the nursery. Shells, buckets, spades, flags and other seaside objects can be placed in the sand and played with. A wood can be created using corrugated paper tree trunks and leaves made by making green handprints, with bark chippings on the floor with plastic minibeasts hidden amongst them.

Collections of objects in the role play area can lead to a range of explorations. The water trough can be used to explore which seaside objects float and sink and how they look different when wet than dry. A collection of leaves or seeds can be explored and sorted according to similarities and differences. A collection of plastic minibeasts can lead to exploration in the garden as to where you will find them in real life (under the ground, on the ground, above the ground). Collections are a really a good way of developing exploratory skills and understandings. Children from 3 years of age will play with the collection for a while and remember previous experiences and knowledge about the objects being explored. They will begin to make closer observations, noticing small details and these can be enhanced through magnification and drawn. At 3 years of age, they will still be very tactile in their exploration, using all their senses, but they can be encouraged to observe more closely, noticing major differences and then similarities, so they can sort and group the collection. They will mainly notice differences in shape or size or colour, but as they develop and get older, they will begin to see other characteristics. By the time they are 5 years of age, children will be able to see a number of different characteristics and be able to sort and re-sort the collection. I once gave 4-year-old children a collection of fruit and vegetables to explore and sort (Johnston & Gray, 1999). The criteria for sorting included shape, colour, size, part of the plant, taste, smell and feel. We used sorting hoops to help us and the children overlapped the hoops to accommodate fruit and vegetables that fitted into more than one category.

Photograph 1.2 Three Year olds Playing with Toys (© Emma Jordan)

Case study

In one piece of research with eight Reception children, aged 4 and 5 years of age, I placed a collection of moving toys on a table in the classroom. The toys included,

- Electrical toys, such as a cheeping chick, an electric car, two sound and light balls and a flashing ball;

- Magnetic toys, such as a monkey and an elephant with magnetic body parts, jumping beans, magnetic frogs and magnetic marbles;
- Wind-up toys, such as a spinning aeroplane, a jumping dog, a wobbling rabbit, a mouse, a pecking bird and a roll-over ladybird;
- Spinning toys, such as a magnetic gyroscope, electrical spinning top, two gyroscopes and a propeller;
- Toys that use air to move, such as a jumping frog and a jumping spider (who move when air in a bulb is squeezed into their legs), a pop gun and a snake (whose tongue sticks out when it is squeezed);
- Other toys, such as a slinky, pecking chicks (who peck when a ball attached to them with string is moved), a sprung jumping man (who jumps up after being pushed down onto a sucker) and a trapeze artist and monkey (who somersault when the wooden sides of the trapeze are squeezed).

The children eagerly began to play with the toys, although they were rather static in their play and did not move from their seats, even if they dropped a toy on the floor, appearing to be worried that they would be reprimanded for doing so. In this initial play activity, the children made many observations about the toys, although most were affective (motivational) in nature, accompanied by comments and exclamations such as *'Oh'*, *'Wow!'* or squeals and giggles. They also interacted socially with their peers, sharing their observations, *'Look what I've got'* and *'Watch'* or demanding a toy from another child with *'Give it to me'*. One child who was playing with a spider who moved when air was squeezed into its legs involved another child in his play with, *'I'm going to get you'*. Two of the children made functional observations and comments about how the toy worked, such as *'When I squash it, it sticks down'* but only one child asked an exploratory question; a question that could lead to further exploration, by asking, *'Why's this not working?'*

I then asked each child to tell me about their toy and how it worked. In the following extract of their explanations, you can see that I tend to dominate the conversation and the children answer the question with little elaboration and no detailed explanation.

Jane:	*What can you tell me about your toy?*
Darren:	*When I squash my toy sticks its tongue out (squeezy snake)*
Jane to Girl 2:	*What can you tell me about your spider?*
Girl 2:	*When I do this (squeezes it) it goes . . . mumbles)*
Darren:	*I've got a bird now – I've got a bird. You wind it up and then push it on the ground and . . . (wind up bird)*

Case study—Cont'd

Jane:	Oh, *you wind it up.*
Darren:	*It's very very clever isn't it?*
Jane to Elisha:	*What can you tell me about your frog (jumping frog)*
Elisha:	*When I do that, it goes out and jumps when you squeeze it*
Jane:	*It jumps when you squeeze it? Why does it jump when you squeeze it?*
Elisha:	*. . . (mumbles) I like it when it jumps!*
Jane:	*You like it when it jumps? What comes out of it when it jumps?*
Elisha:	*. . . the legs*
Jane:	*The legs come out? Wonderful!*
Darren:	*You have to do this to make the wheel work (holding up the magnetic gyroscope)*
Jane:	*You have to do that? Tell me about it?*
Darren:	*This is what you do and when it comes to the end it bounces*
Jane:	*So how does it work?*
Darren:	*You do it over here first (holding it up) and it goes down and when it gets here (pointing to the bottom of the tracks) it goes down and down*
Jane:	*It bounces*

Finally, the children sorted the toys into groups chosen by them. The groups they chose were,

1 Balls/ round
2 Yellow
3 Green
4 Black
5 Wind up hoop

Reflection for early career professional

- How do you think you could build upon the children's enthusiasm and move them towards exploration of the toys?
- What interactions/ questions do you think would support and encourage exploration?

⇨

- How could you move the children from the use of categoric groups for sorting (shape, colour, etc) to more functional and exploratory groups?

Reflection for leader/ manager

- Review the activities you provide for the children in your setting. How do they encourage motivational exploration?
- What other activities could support exploration? How?
- Analyse the way in which you and your staff/ colleagues interact with children to support exploration. How could this be improved?

Between the ages of 3 and 5 years of age, children will have greater understanding of the world and will build on this in their explorations. Their ideas and understandings will be different from those of older children and adults as they are still based on limited experience. They are also increasingly well researched (e.g. Fleer, 2007) and this research has shown us that sometimes their experiences lead them to personal, and incorrect theories about the world (Mayall, 2007). For example, many young children believe that heavy objects fall faster than light ones or heavy objects will sink and light ones will float. Even when challenged, they will find some way to cling to their personal theory and will tell you that you have made an object heavier by changing its shape. Reiss & Tunnicliffe's (2002) research of children's drawings of the human body show how early ideas based on observation and exploration, combine with taught ideas to create some interesting alternative conceptions about internal structures and functions.

It is also at this age that children's enthusiasm for explorations and investigation can be developed or crushed and it is a fairly fine line between encouraging them in their exploration and keeping them safe (Palmer, 2006). If children are to develop enquiring minds and understandings about the world that will help them in their daily lives they need to be encouraged in their early explorations and discoveries. For example, as future citizens, they need to be able to explore the environment, understand and enjoy the environment and make environmental decisions about waste disposal, recycling etc. This does not happen if their enthusiasm for exploration is curbed at an early age.

Transition to Key Stage 1 (5 to 7 years of age)

Transition from the Early Years Foundation Stage to Key Stage 1, should not be a step, but a gentle slope. Children should be unaware of the differences between the two stages and continue to develop their understandings about the world by moving from the familiar and local to the more unfamiliar and further afield. This can be hindered by the different curricula in the two stages, with the Early Years Foundation Stage being a skills-based, child-centred and practical curriculum and Key Stage 1 being a subject-focused, knowledge-based and teacher-led curriculum. This can make exploration and investigation more difficult and it is important to focus on quality exploration of the world which leads to understanding, rather than the imposition of knowledge which is not understood and is easily forgotten.

When children move into Key Stage 1, they should continue to explore the world around them and be encouraged to use these explorations to plan further explorations and investigations. If these plans arise out of their explorations and are decided by them, with support from their teachers, they will be well-matched to their learning needs and help to keep them motivated and focused. They can test out ideas in an investigative way, controlling variables and measuring results. They can test the strength of different papers, the way different substances mix with water, the effect of exercise on their bodies (pulse and breathing). They can investigate what happens to toys left out in the rain or different objects when put in water. They can compare their environment with those further afield, through use of internet links, video conferencing with other schools abroad, using freely available software. They can use a travelling bear (see the Barnaby Bear website http://www.barnaby-bear.co.uk/ and the Geographical Association website http://www.geography.org.uk/)

In the move towards investigating, children will need to be supported to ensure that the plans they make are realistic and achievable, that they have the skills and knowledge to control variables, take measurements, predict and interpret their findings. This may mean that greater structure is needed to support them in the early stages of the investigations, but that opportunities are provided to practice their skills and discuss their ideas.

Supporting the development of exploration and investigation

In supporting the development of exploration and investigation, professionals need to remember two of the main principles of the Early Years Foundation Stage (DCSF, 2008: 5) concerning learning and development that *'children develop and learn in different ways and at different rates and all areas of Learning and Development are equally important and inter-connected'*. Earlier in this chapter we discussed the differences ages make to children's exploration and touched upon the different interests and experiences they have which influence their ability to make sense of the world around them. Here we discuss the important factors that support then while they explore and investigate,

- the importance of providing a rich learning environment;
- the resources used to support exploration and investigation;
- opportunities for children to interact with each other;
- the importance of the adult professional support;
- the support the home can provide.

Before we look at each of these factors in turn, we will look at an holistic role play, which considers the two principles of learning and development in the Early Years Foundation Stage (DCSF, 2008), that is the individual and the cross-curricular nature of learning. In this role play a building site was set up in the classroom, with a balance beam, large bricks, cardboard boxes of different sizes, PE mats, clipboards, paper and pencils (to draw plans). The learning objectives for the role play were,

Communication, Language and Literacy:
    Communication with other children;
    Vocabulary (describing materials in their own words, introduction of new words
        where appropriate e.g. sand, brick, build, stable, safe, climb).

Mathematical Development:
    Counting and sorting building materials.

Physical Development:
    Building structures;
    Climbing and balancing.

Personal, Social and Emotional Development:
  Social interaction, taking turns.

Creative Development:
  Drawing plans of building.

At first there is little obvious development in Knowledge and Understanding of the World, but the actual play of one child took a different pathway. Drew enthusiastically went into the building site and after collaboratively building a house with other children, he went to the other side of the room and took two long lengths of material; one green and one orange. He wrapped himself up in the green material, so that just his head emerged from the folds. He then wriggled around the building site being a caterpillar. After a while, he covered his head with the material and lay quietly in the middle of the building site, with the other children playing around him and announced that he was now *'turning into a butterfly'*. Finally, Drew got the orange length of material and intertwining it with the green emerged out of the cocoon he had made as a butterfly and then flittered around the building site.

In this play Drew was drawing upon his knowledge and understanding of the life cycle of a butterfly (taken from his previous experiences and the book *'The Hungry Caterpillar'* (Carle, 1970). So in his play, Drew was linking development in physical and creative development with knowledge and understanding of the world and literacy.

Practical tasks

Plan and set up a cross-curricular play activity for the children in your care. Evaluate the activity and identify how successful it was in,

- developing the children's knowledge and understanding of the world;
- linking different areas of the Early Years Foundation Stage;
- building on individual children's experiences and ideas.

The learning environment

A learning environment that encourages curiosity, enquiry and exploration; an *'enabling environment'* (DCSF, 2008: 5), will motivate children and support their development in this key area of the Early Years Foundation Stage. Since exploration is very sensual at this stage, the environment needs to have lots of sensory stimuli; things to see, smell, hear, feel and taste, where safe. Each sense can be emphasized or focused on by closing eyes, so that smells, tastes, sounds and the way things feel are more obvious. Children with sensory impairments will often have their other senses heightened and this can be emphasized, by creating an environment with additional sensory experiences.

Indoors

Indoors, the classroom should be an environment that encourages exploration and curiosity, through interactive displays, with motivating objects to touch and explore. Feely boxes, unusual objects, bright colours, sounds, etc. will all stimulate the children to want to find out more about them. A questioning environment is also important. This is one where the children feel safe to enquire and ask questions and the professional encourages enquiry by asking questions of themselves and with the children. Too many activities can lead to sensory overload and activities which are overused or put out too often can demotivate. With very young children it is sometimes best to plan the environment so that there are opportunities for familiar play, as well as new and novel experiences. This is because sometimes looking at something in a different way can be very motivating and can encourage new lines of exploration.

Outside

The outside environment is rich in opportunities for exploring the world and developing knowledge about it. Even if the outside play area in your setting is concrete and bricks, there are plenty of avenues for exploration. Plants growing and minibeasts hiding in cracks and brickwork can be observed. Drying puddles and shadows can be explored. Messy play, water play, painting, etc., can be set up outside and role play areas can be introduced, such as a garden shed, building site, car wash, jungle, etc.

Walks along the street can identify many opportunities for exploration. Children can collect leaves, stones, feathers and other items of interest and take them back to explore further. One street can provide many opportunities, with plants, animals, weather, weathering, a pond, a park or garden to be observed. A baker's shop can lead to explorations of baking, a supermarket of growing fruit and vegetables, washing powders or a pizza shop of pizza toppings.

The age and construction of different buildings can be explored and the age and jobs of inhabitants be identified. Some schools make great use of the outside classroom and the increase in 'forest schools' recognizes the importance of the outdoor environment in supporting learning and development.

Reflection for early career professional

Look at the indoor environment that you provide for children from a child's perspective.

- How could you change the environment to make it more encouraging for exploration and investigation?
- How could you use familiar activities and phenomena and encourage further exploration?

Look also at the local environment and identify opportunities for exploration to develop knowledge and understanding of the world.

- How could you make better use of the local environment to develop opportunities for cross-curricular exploration?

Reflection for leader/ manager

Consider the indoor environment in your setting. Discuss with your staff/ colleagues as to what features encourage exploration and what features inhibit exploration. Decide how you can develop all areas of the setting to support exploration and investigation.

As a staff, consider how you could make better use of the local environment and the environment further afield. Plan ways to develop your outside play facilities and make better use of the community and locality surrounding your setting to maximize opportunities for exploration.

Resources

Earlier in this section we discussed the importance of managing the activities and resources available to children, so that they remain motivated and curious about the world around them. It is important that resources captivate interest in the children. There are also a number of resources that can support children's exploration, by enhancing observations. These include magnifiers and digital microscopes for enhancing visual observations; slide projectors can also be used to make small objects larger (by making slides of them) so that small features can be seen and drawn. Paint colour charts can aid visual recognition of the different shades of colour in the environment. Stethoscopes, tape/ CD recorders and video recorders can help to capture sounds and sequences of sounds. Crayon rubbings can accentuate patterns on bricks, bark, grates, etc. Video-conferencing can link children to other parts of the world. Sometimes the use of resources to enhance observations can detract from the exploration as the children focus on the magnifier, stethoscope, etc., rather than the object to be observed (Johnston, 2005). In some ways this does not matter as exploring the resources is an important step to being able to use them properly in the future.

Interaction with other children and professionals

Photograph 1.3 Exploring with others; adults and peers (© P. Hopkins)

Exploration is supported through peer interaction, where children have the opportunity to discuss their ideas, listen to the ideas of others. In the case study above with children aged 4 and 5 years of age, one of the main findings is that the children's interactions provide the main source of support for explanations of their findings. However, the support of all the professionals is also important to introduce new and correct vocabulary, pose open-ended questions (Johnston, 2005; DCSF, 2008), to motivate children and to encourage more sophisticated thinking and further exploration.

At this age, we need to be very careful to ensure that the experiences we provide for children and the way we interact with them; that is the pedagogical approaches we use, support their explorations (see Venaille, et. al, 2003; Shayer & Adey 2002). However care is needed to ensure that this interaction does not perpetuate alternative conceptions rather than developing learning. For example, we often explore growing plants with no mention of the part played by air in their growth and this makes it difficult to understand photosynthesis later in their scientific development.

A review of research into pedagogical approaches in early years science (BERA, 2003) found that a constructivist approach to teaching and learning, developed after the SPACE (Science Process and Concept Exploration) research in the 1990s, had not been effectively implemented with young children. Early exploratory skills and understandings will not just 'emerge' through discussion of experiences and children need well-planned practical and play experiences to support their development (Moyles, 2005; DCSF, 2008). Such exploratory experiences are likely to support holistic development, as they treat cognitive, social and emotional development as complementary (Siraj-Blatchford et. al, 2002). In this way effective learning involves interaction between children, their environment and adults, with children exercising some autonomy and developing understanding from experiences which build upon their previous knowledge.

Practical tasks

Plan an exploratory learning activity for your children, that incorporates both peer and adult interaction.

Carry out and evaluate the activity and identify how successful it was in developing the children's knowledge and understanding of the world.

- How important was the peer interaction in the success of the activity?
- How did your interaction support the children's learning?
- How could you improve your interaction to further develop the children's learning and your practice?
- How did the children feel about the activity? Did they learn best from the peer or adult interaction?

Home support for exploration and investigation

There is concern that modern life has an adverse effect on children's ability to explore (Palmer, 2006), as parents are often stressed by modern life and self-absorbed by their own concerns, anxieties and feelings (Elkind, 2001) and do not spend quality time with their children. This can result in weak cognitive development (Gerhardt, 2004), exacerbated by excess sugar and processed food. The result is that family life does not support quality interaction and children's exploration.

Children who have quality interactions with their parents or carers and who have opportunities to explore their own world and other localities with them are greatly advantaged. Many family members have interests and expertise that supports children's knowledge and understanding of the world, such as the parent who is a keen gardener or baker, or the family member who is an electrician, wine maker, builder, or mechanic. In early years settings we can utilize family members' interests and knowledge to extend children's experiences of the world (DCSF, 2008).

Reflection for early career professional

- How do you think you could utilize family interests and expertise more effectively?
- What interests and expertise would complement your own to help children's exploratory activities?

Reflection for Leader/ Manager

Undertake a family audit to discover what skills, interests and expertise the carers and parents of your children have which could enhance your provision.

- How do you and your colleagues/ staff feel about using parents/ carers to support your provision?
- What roles/ activities do you feel able to use parents and carers in a supportive role?

Plan how you can make better use of parents'/ carers' expertise. Try one or more idea out and evaluate the impact on children's learning and development.

References

Ainsworth, M., Blehar, M., Waters, E. and Wall, S (1978) *Patterns of Attachment*. Hillsdale NJ: Erlbaum.

BERA, (2003) *Early Years Research: Pedagogy, Curriculum and Adult Roles, Training and Professionalism*. Southwell, Notts: BERA.

Carle, E. (1970) *The Very Hungry Caterpillar*. Harmondsworth: Penguin.

DCSF, (2008) *The Early Years Foundation Stage; Setting the Standard for Learning, Development and Care for Children from Birth to Five; Practice Guidance*. London: DCSF.

de Bóo, M. (2004) *The Curriculum Partnership: Early Years Handbook*. Sheffield: Geography Association.

DES (1967) *Children and their Primary School. A report of the Central Advisory Council for Education (England) Vol. 1: Report*. London: HMSO.

Elkind, D. (2001) *The Hurried Child. Growing Up Too Fast Too Soon* 3rd *Edition*. Cambridge, MA: Da Capio Press.

Fleer, M. (ed) (2007) *Young Children: Thinking About the Scientific World. Early Childhood Australia*: Watson, ACT (also available at www.earlychildhoodaustralia.org.au

Gerhardt, S. (2004) *Why Love Matters; How Affection Shapes A Baby's Brain*. London: Routledge.

Johnston, J. (2004) The Value of Exploration and Discovery, *Primary Science Review*. 85: 21–23.

Johnston, J. (2005) *Early Explorations in Science* 2nd *Edition*. Maidenhead: Open University Press.

Johnston, J. and Gray, A. (1999) *Enriching Early Scientific Learning*. Buckingham: Open University Press.

Johnston, J. and Nahmad-Williams, L. (2008) *Early Childhood Studies*. Harlow: Pearsons.

Kallery, M. and Psillos, D. (2002) What happens in the early years science classroom? The reality of teachers' curriculum implementation activities. *European Early Childhood Education Research Journal*, 10(2), 49–61.

Maslow, A. H. (1968) *Towards a Psychology of Being*. Princeton, NJ: D. Van Nostrand Co.

Mayall, B. (2007) 'Children's Lives Outside School and their Educational Impact', *Primary Review Research Briefings 8/1*. http://www.primaryreview.org.uk/Downloads/Int_Reps/3.Children_lives_voices/Primary_Review_8–1_briefing_Children_s_lives_outside_school_071123.pdf

Montessori, M. (1912) *The Montessori Method*. London: Heinemann.

Moyles, J. R. (ed.) (2005) *The Excellence of Play* 2nd *Edition*. Maidenhead: Open University Press.

National Research Council of the National Academies (2007) *Taking Science to School*. Washington, DC: The National Academies Press.

Palmer, S. (2006) *Toxic Childhood. How the Modern World is Damaging our Children and What We Can Do about it*. London: Orion.

Reiss, M. and Tunnicliffe, S. D. (2002) 'An International Study of Young People's Drawings of What is Inside Themselves' *Journal of Biological Education*. 36(2): 58–64.

Shayer, M. and Adey, P. (2002) (eds.) *Learning Intelligence. Cognitive Acceleration Across the Curriculum from 5 to 15 Years*. Buckingham, Open University Press.

Siraj-Blatchford, I., Sylva, K., Muttock, S,, Gilden, R. and Bell, D. (2002) *Researching Effective Pedagogy in the Early Years.* London: DfES.

Venaille, G., Adey, P., Larkin, S., Robertson, A., Hammersmith, F. (2003) 'Fostering Thinking Through Science in the Early Years of Schooling' *International Journal of Science Education* 25(11): 1313–1331.

2 Designing and Making

Chapter Outline

Introduction

Design and making, the early years is the fore-runner of design and technology in primary education and it involves the interconnection of two components (Richie, 2001). Design is the *fusion of innovation, function, aesthetics, ergonomics (concerning the physical relationships between humans and machines), environmental considerations, communication and visual identity* (Richie, 2001: 5). Technology or making in the early years, is *the science and art of getting things done through the application of knowledge* (Richie, 2001: 6); making things using the knowledge we have of the world around us. Designing and making involves many cross curricular and generic knowledge, skills and attitudes. Technical skills involved in making include the ability to join together, construct, measure and handle tools. Intellectual skills involved in designing and problem-solving include the ability to model ideas mentally, questioning, hypothesizing and analyzing, synthesizing and interpreting skills; the skills needed to think critically. However without (Johnston, 2005):

- motivational attitudes such as enthusiasm, curiosity, interest and motivation,
- behavioural attitudes such as creativity, inventiveness and objectivity,
- reflective attitudes such as open-mindedness, tentativeness and a respect for evidence.

Technical and intellectual skills are unlikely to develop.

Designing and making involves motivating practical activities and challenges children's understanding and in this way it helps to develop skills, attitudes and understandings. There are specific understandings related to design and technology, such as knowledge and understanding of materials and components (DfEE, 1999) and how they can use materials and components to create and make and solve problems. In addition, there are cross curricular and generic understandings and skills about the wider world around them that children can bring to their designing and making, use to solve problems and develop in a cross-curricular way. For example children can use and develop mathematical skills and understandings, measuring, calculating, using number, shape, volume, weight and size. They can use and develop literacy skills as they communicate and evaluate with others about their designs and creations. They can draw, write and record plans and ideas in a variety of visual and digital ways, using information technology (IT). Children can also develop general thinking skills enabling them to handle conflicts and make decisions when planning, designing and making. They can use and develop scientific skills through exploring how things work and in making simple technological objects, such as moving vehicles, moving toys etc. In this way designing and making has a number of distinct features as it,

- builds upon previous development,
- is highly interactive, involving children in interacting with ideas, resources, each other and adults,
- is cross-curricular in nature;
- supports the more creative and technological learners, as opposed to more didactic teaching.

The development of designing and making

The Early Years Foundation Stage (DCSF, 2008) identifies that children's knowledge and understanding of the world can develop through and be developed by three of the four themed principles: Positive Relationships, Enabling

Environments and Learning and Development. However the first theme, a Unique Child is also valid (see also Chapter 1, Exploration and Investigation) as children can learn through designing and making about themselves as individuals; how to be confident, self-assured and resilient. Through interaction with the world around them and with their peers and adults, they can develop social skills and positive relationships. They can explore how things work in the world around them, thus stimulating their curiosity and interest in how things work or why something happens. This is best done in an *enabling environment* (DCSF, 2008) that stimulates and encourages curiosity through practical experiences that '*encourage exploration, experimentation, observation, problem solving, prediction, critical thinking, decision making and discussion*' (DCSF, 2008: 78).

Designing and making from birth to 3 years of age

In Chapter 1, Exploring and Investigating, we looked at the way children develop understanding about the world around them. As they explore, they will learn about a range of different materials; wood, stone, textiles, metal, rubber, plastics, through the use of all their senses. They will learn that different materials are used to make different objects and begin to be curious as to why some materials are better than others for specific purposes. They will learn that woolly textiles are good at keeping them warm in cold weather, that a rubber ball bounces better than a textile ball and that grass or soft matting is less harmful when they fall than concrete. They learn that metal objects feel colder than wooden objects, fleece or felt is soft and cuddly and finger paint is squelchy and moist. When using simple cutlery they will learn that the shape of a spoon is best for picking up liquids and fork prongs are good for spiking lumps of food.

Curiosity (as discussed in Chapter 1, Exploring and Investigating) is an important aspect of learning about the world and an essential pre-requisite to designing and making. As children play with toys, they may be curious as to how they work, look closely at mechanisms and repeat actions time and again, apparently to help them understand how things work and to perfect action. Toy cars get rolled and they learn by looking and by trial and error that the wheels will enable the car to roll. At home, they will enjoy operating simple household mechanisms, such as flushing toilets, television remote controls and light switches and for this reason we have to ensure their safety by not allowing them access to 'unsafe' objects and mechanisms and supervising their use of others. They particularly enjoy playing with objects that they see adults using, such as mobile phones, computers, vacuum cleaners, etc. Replica, toy household objects can enable children to play at being adults, but while role play should be encouraged, replicas that imitate real mechanisms can stifle creativity and will not necessarily encourage curiosity. It is better to allow children to use some real mechanisms with support and look at how things work with them. They can then make their own replicas using whatever resources they can find. A wooden brick can become a mobile phone and the children can draw the keys and the microphone. A large packaging box can become a washing machine and the children can decide how to create an opening door and a spinning wheel; maybe with a washing up bowl or a sieve or salad spinner inside. A cooker can be created out of another large cardboard box and the children can decide how to add doors, hot plates and controls.

Case study

The clock in the day nursery was not working and so Dawn, the professional in charge of the 2 to 3 year old room, was late in preparing the children's milk and fruit snack. The clock was taken off the wall to await a new battery and later, after the snack, Joel (aged 2 and a half years) picked up the clock looking at it intently, turning it over to see the battery and wires on the back. He took a sheet of card and drew a clock face on it, again looking at the clock to make sure he got the numbers in the correct place. He then turned the card over and drew the battery and wires on the back. He then went to Dawn and said *'It's alright now as I have made a new clock'*, and showed Dawn the clock that he had constructed and explained how it worked. Dawn put it on the wall next to the space vacated by the clock. Later, when Dawn had found a new battery, she asked Joel if he would like to put it into the clock. A small group of children watched and they talked about what would happen when the new battery was inserted and then looked at the second hand of the clock as it began to move. Dawn then moved the hour and minute hands so the clock was correct and put it back on the wall. Joel was a bit disappointed that his clock now did not tell the correct time and Dawn got him to add hands that pointed to snack time so he and all the other children would be able to know when snack time was by comparing with the 'real' clock.

Case study—Cont'd

Reflection for early career professional

- How else could Dawn encourage Joel and the other children to use this opportunity for designing and making?
- How could you ensure your learning environment is one that provides opportunities for designing and making for the under three-year-olds?
- How can you change your planning and practice to encourage more designing and making activities?

Reflection for leader/ manager

- How does the learning environment in your setting encourage designing and making opportunities?
- How could you develop the learning environment to encourage designing and making activities?
- How knowledgeable are the staff in your setting at supporting and encouraging designing and making development?

Creative collage activities can allow children to design their own pictures and patterns using different materials. Animal pictures can be created using raw wool for sheep, strips of old (or faux) leather for cows and clear sequins for fish scales. Small pieces of tissue paper screwed up, strips of paper curled and shredded paper can all be used to create differing effects. Wool can be woven or plaited; beads can be threaded onto laces to make patterns; finger paint can be used with sand or gravel to create different textures and patterns.

As children play in the sand or water tray they can solve simple problems, trying to make boats that float or sink, or build a big sand castle with wet or dry sand. When playing with duplo bricks, children can be asked to build the tallest tower or make a bridge to go between two tables. When blowing bubbles, children can be challenged to blow the biggest bubble or the most bubbles in one blow. When playing with toy cars, they can be challenged to make the car go faster or further. As children develop, the problems can move from the familiar and exploratory and become more specific and challenging. It is however important that the level of challenge is correct. Too great and the children become frustrated; too little and they become bored. Challenge is a great motivator. Problem solving activities can be made more difficult by the complexity of the challenge, the context in which they are set and the level of conceptual understanding needed to solve the problem. So simple problems posed while the children play are often best for young children, especially open-ended play problems that have a number of possible solutions.

Designing and making from 3 to 5 years of age

As children develop they will increasingly move from the very familiar to the less familiar contexts as they explore the world around them. They may be taken on trips to play park and experience the way of using the swings, roundabout and slide. They may go on holidays to different locations and experience new mechanisms, such as tractors, peddle-boats, canal locks, bridges or buses. As Siraj-Blatchford (2001: 2) says, '*it is important that we provide*' children '*with the essential early experiences that they must have if they are to go on to understand scientific and technological explanations later.*' As discussed in Chapter 1, Exploring and Investigating, this is still much more about exploration, the haphazard and ad hoc use of all their senses to learn about the world they inhabit, rather than the more systematic investigation, more suitable for older children. However, they will also increasingly solve simple problems and learn to use simple tools, through a more systematic exploration and practice. There are arguments for the use of 'safe' tools, such as blunt knives and scissors or rubber hammers and plastic spanners, although Steiner education (see Nichol, 2007) advocates the use of 'real' tools as safer and more supportive of future development. It is much easier to use a sharp, metal pair of scissors than to use a blunt, plastic pair and it is much easier to cut an apple or even a banana with a sharp knife, rather than a blunt one. Children do need to be shown how to use tools safely, but once shown they will practise and perfect. It is also important to consider what the progression in the use of tools is and to plan both the type of tool and its use (Hope, 2006). I have used a large tool box filled with children's sized 'real' tools such as hammers, screwdrivers, spanners, sandpaper, etc., as well as a selected set of nails, screws, rawl plugs, etc. The children are asked to sort the tool box. As they do this they have the opportunity to use the tools and can be encouraged to look for use of the different screws, nails, etc., in the construction of the building they are in (see Johnston & Herridge, 2004). On one occasion as small Reception aged child (aged 4 to 5 years), who was identified by his teacher as having behavioural difficulties, spent a long time quietly sorting the tolls and components. I posed a small problem for him to solve, by asking him why he thought we used screws rather than nails in construction. He spent some time looking at the use of screws and nails in the construction of different things in the classroom, such as cupboards, display boards and in hanging doors and later he told me why screws were used to hang the doors in his classroom, rather than large nails and why we needed to have door hinges.

Problem-solving activities can use fiction, fantasy or stories as starting points (Siraj-Blatchford & MacLeod-Brudenell, 1999; Howe, et. al., 2001; Johnston, 2005). For example, the *Three Little Pigs* story can lead to designing and making 'wolf-proof' houses; *Jim and the Beanstalk* (Briggs, 1970) can lead to designing and making wigs or teeth for the giant; *Mr Bebleman's Bakery* (Green, 1978) can lead to designing and making your own bread.

Young children will also use a range of small and large construction kits which can help them as they develop gross and fine motor skills as well as understanding of construction (see Johnston & Nahmad-Williams, 2008). Large and small wooden bricks, duplo and lego, sets of gears, connecting straws and 2-dimensional connecting shapes, will all support their ability to make and construct and develop their fine motor skills, enabling them to make increasingly more complex constructions. When given simple construction problems, such as how can you make a 'wolf-proof' house, the children will have to design, choose materials and use tools with a specific purpose in mind. In the case study below, the problem solving, designing and making elements of Designing and Making (DCSF, 2008) are incorporated into one role play activity which illustrates how children from 3 to 5 years of age develop their skills and understandings.

Case study

In one Foundation Stage classroom, a building site was set up for the children. This consisted of,

- a design section, with the computer with simple design/ construction software, a table with clipboards, paper and pencils for designing and small construction bricks, so mock ups could be made and presented,

- a large wooden brick construction set and a collection of cardboard boxes,
- a construction table with simple tools (hammers, screwdrivers, card scissors), components (nails, screws, glue) and materials (wood, thick card, etc.),
- hard hats, reflective clothing and boiler suits and toy tools like drills, spades, forks, etc.

The children were encouraged use of the area to role play, developing understanding of designing and making. A small group of Early Years Foundation Stage children (aged 3 years) began to use the large bricks to make a construction. Ashley took the toy drill and started to *'fix'* the bricks together to make the tower *'safer'* (see Photograph 2.1). When the tower started to wobble, Suzie and Freddy decided to make the *'bottom with big bricks and the top with little ones'* to make it safer. Some of the older children (aged 4 years) decided to construct a house with small lego on the design table. Diara started by drawing a design of their house and showed how different types of lego should be used for different parts of the house. Later he constructed his house to his own design.

Photograph 2.1 Role play in the building site

Reflection for early career professional

- What other role play activities could support designing and making in 3 to 5 year olds?
- How could you develop the children at different stages within the Early Years Foundation Stage to move from simple construction to design and construction?

Case study—Cont'd

Reflection for leader/ manager

- What is the progression of skills and understandings in designing and making in the 3 to 5 year olds in your setting?
- How can you develop the provision of activities in your setting to develop these skills and understandings?

Transition to Key Stage 1 (5 to 7 years of age)

When children enter Key Stage 1, they will continue on the pathway from the familiar to the unfamiliar. They will be continuing to plan, design, work with tools and construct and in addition they will increasingly discuss, communicate and evaluate. The National Curriculum divides Design and Technology into 3 sections (DfEE, 1999).

- Developing, planning and communicating ideas.
- Working with tools, equipment, materials and components to make quality products.
- Evaluating processes and products.

Children will still be exploring materials using their own senses and there is clearly a link here with Materials and the Properties (Sc3) in the science national curriculum (DfEE, 1999). However in Design and Technology, children use the term materials in a different way, focusing on the wide range of materials available, rather than the scientific way of focusing on states of matter (solid, liquid, gases) or the everyday focus of textiles (Johnston, 2005). In Design and Technology, children will be exploring the properties and uses of a wide range of materials. When developing, planning and communicating ideas, children will be involved in making their own plans, using their own experiences as springboards for ideas, but also using ideas generated by others. Importantly they will be discussing their ideas with others and increasingly working cooperatively and collaboratively. They may design celebration cards for members of their family and discuss the sorts of design that would suit the recipient. They will be able to design pizza toppings or fruit milkshakes and then make their pizza or milkshake and evaluate it themselves and by sharing with their peers. When working with tools, equipment, materials and components they should be able to choose the best tool for the task they have to do and choose the best materials to make it from. This may mean that when making a bridge they choose what material to use to make the bridge they have designed (suspension bridge, span bridge, arch bridge, cantilever bridge, pontoon) and the tools they need to make the bridge.

In making their bridges or other structures or technological items, for example, a musical instrument, a machine to sort balls, or an insulated house, (see Wilson, 2009) children will need to make measurements, mark out, cut and shape a range of materials (DfEE, 1999). They will then assemble the components to make the finished product, (DfEE, 1999) and ensure a good finish. Finally, they can evaluate the finished product. When evaluating the product, it is important that the criteria for evaluation are clearly communicated before the design stage, as this will ensure all are working towards the same success criteria. With a bridge, this may be the design, the span and supporting a specific mass. With a musical instrument, it could be the sound it makes and the design/ aesthetics. With a ball-sorting machine, it could be the number of different balls it sorts, the accuracy of sorting and the creativity of design. With an insulated house, it could be the design of the house and the effectiveness of the insulation. If we also want children to develop cooperative or collaborative skills, communicating with and learning from each other, we can add success criteria like ability to work together, perseverance, or enthusiasm for the group task and get children to collaborate on designing and making. In this way we will be encouraging children to be creative and collaborative and fulfilling many of the requirements of the primary strategy (DfES, 2003).

Case study

In the summer term in one nursery and infant school, the Key Stage 1 children were planning a Teddy Bears' picnic for the Foundation Stage to familiarize them with Key Stage 1, in preparation for their transition in the following term. The children work together to plan a menu, prepare party food, with due consideration to safety and hygiene. They prepare resources for food production and for the party (tables, chairs, rugs), design, make and send out invitations and decide roles (food preparation, table design and layout, servers, etc). They take photographs at the picnic and the Foundation Stage children send them letters to thank them, identifying the 'best' parts of the picnic. The children use both the photographs, letters and their own experience of the picnic to evaluate the success of the day, and identify whether they should have another one next year and what they could have done differently.

Reflection for early career professional

Look at the curriculum for designing and making in the early Years Foundation Stage (DCSF, 2008) and design and technology at Key Stage 1 (DfEE, 1999) and consider,

- What are the major differences between the two curricula and what problems may children encounter as they move from one stage of learning to the other?
- How could you use design and make activities to span the gap between the Early Years Foundation Stage and Key Stage 1?

Reflection for leader/ manager

As a team in your school or setting, look at the curriculum for designing and making in the early Years Foundation Stage (DCSF, 2008) and design and technology at Key Stage 1 and Key Stage 2 (DfEE, 1999) and consider,

- How do children progress in design and making understandings and skills through the Early Years Foundation Stage, Key Stage 1 and Key Stage 2?
- How you can ease children's transition through whole school/setting design and make activities?
- How could you also incorporate the home, parents/ carers and the wider community in these activities?

Supporting development in designing and making

There are two main considerations that professionals need to make in order to support children in designing and making, the creation of a rich learning environment and the approach to learning and teaching employed to support development.

Enabling environments

Designing and making requires a rich and stimulating learning environment, that allows the children the *'time and free access to the tools, instruments and materials that they require to investigate, design and make for themselves'* (Siraj-Blatchford & MacLeod-Brudenell, 1999: 87). Resources should be stored in ways that children can locate and choose ones that are appropriate to them and the project they are engaged in and Siraj-Blatchford & MacLeod-Brudenell recommend organizing resources under broad themes, such as craft tools, materials, art materials, etc. You could get the children to consider the design of the classroom and the location of resources to make access and use easy. In some settings, resources may be centrally stored rather than in individual classrooms and then not only the ease of access, but the safe return and tidying up of resources needs to be considered.

The environment also needs to be stimulating so that it encourages the children's interest (see also Chapter 1, Exploring and Investigating). Interactive displays of a range of mechanisms that children can observe and take apart (Sweet, 1996) to explore how they work can stimulate children, as can small problem-solving activities or evaluation activities. When buying a range of moving toys (see Chapter 1, Exploring and Investigating), I try and buy two, one to play with and one to take apart and see how it works. For example, opening up a musical spinning top shows a fascinating mechanism, using spinning forces (centrifugal forces), which forces a small ball bearing to join two metal strips and complete a circuit, looking inside a wind up toy or a pull back toy will also show how the mechanism works. It is not necessary for the children to completely understand the way mechanisms work, but what is important is that they feel able in the learning environment to explore and speculate and come up with their own answers based on their exploration.

Most importantly, children need time in the learning environment, not just to 'do' or 'make', but also to 'experience' and 'think' and communicate ideas to adults and their peers. In a rich learning environment, the children are not rushed from one activity to another, so that coverage is achieved. Rather the whole curriculum is considered in a more holistic and relevant way and with spaces for thinking about, talking about and making sense of experiences. In this way, we are recognizing that in designing and making there are many cross-curricular and generic skills and understandings involved. So children involved in the Teddy Bear's picnic, described in the case study above, will be developing in personal, social, emotional and physical areas as well as learning about designing and making.

Learning approaches

In the early years, children need to be tactile and involved in first hand experiences (DCSF, 2008). There are strong beliefs, borne out by research (Siraj-Blatchford and Siraj-Blatchford, 1998) that this should involve some form of instruction. In research studying 5-year-olds ability to use construction sets effectively, Siraj-Blatchford and Siraj-Blatchford (1998) found that direct instruction was more effective than discovery methods. In other contexts, I have argued (Johnston, 2004), that discovery learning has often been misunderstood and that effective discovery is supported, in a similar way to Blatchford's instruction, through modelling, questioning and scaffolding learning. Sweet (1996: 278–279) advocates the 'hands off' approach, but identifies some areas where more direct support is necessary through,

- Verbal instruction, or talking through the processes and encouraging children to do something for themselves and thus giving them the satisfaction of doing it themselves.
- Demonstration, showing how to use a tool, so that children can use tools safely or showing them an example of a finished product so they can explore it and see how they think it works or fits together.
- Disassembling, or allowing the children to take something apart to see how it works, or for the professional to show how something works and then disassemble it, so the children can reassemble successfully.
- Giving assistance, such as supporting fine motor skills, where children are finding their fine motor skills are not sufficient to do the job. If they have had a try and need a small amount of help to thread a needle, hold a piece of wood steady, perfect a technique, or produce a more perfect end product, then it is acceptable to give them the support they need.

This supportive approach also involves professionals challenging children to solve simple problems in their familiar play activities, often through simple challenging questions. Some examples of making and doing activities suitable for children in the early years are set out below (see also, Siraj-Blatchford & MacLeod-Brudenell, 1999; de Bóo, 2004: Johnston, 2005).

- Make a plasticine boat which floats. How many marbles can you get in your boat?
- Make a waterproof hat for teddy/make an umbrella. What materials will you need to make the hat/ umbrella?
- Make a marble maze. The marble must travel through a table top maze without being touched. Who can make the slowest marble maze?
- Make a musical instrument. Can you make your instrument play a scale?
- Make some packaging to protect an egg when dropped. Why will this material make be the most helpful in making a package??
- Make the fastest land boat (car with a sail which can be powered with a hair dryer). Why do you think this shaped sail will be the fastest?
- Make some traffic lights. How do the traffic lights work?

The challenges given should not be too great to be frustrating and not too simple to be boring for the children. This is often best done in an open-ended approach where the children make decisions for themselves about how to solve a problem, how to start, proceed and evaluate. Where approaches are open-ended, the children will enter the activity at an appropriate level and make decisions for themselves about what they can and need to know and what they can and need to do.

Practical task – make a box-model vehicle

Start by discussing with the children what sort of vehicle they will make and what resources are needed to make it. The children can begin to collect resources. You may need to show them how to add wheels to their box and so the wheels will turn. This can be done by using card circle (or tin lids or other circular objects as wheels) and fixing them to the box using a small piece of dowel through each 'wheel' and foxed to the box using small cuttings of plastic tubing, that fit the dowel snugly. Wheels can be fixed to axles in the same way and can be fixed to the bottom of the box (so the box sits on the wheels and the axle is fixed and the wheels turn) or

Practical task—Cont'd

through the box so the axle and wheels can turn together (see Figure 2.1). It is often a good idea to have some example for the children to see so they can use them as a guide to make their own. The children may need help fixing the wheels on the box and with cutting out windows and doors on the vehicle, but they should be able to decide how to do it and to decorate/ paint the vehicle to their own design. When painting the box vehicle, if a small amount of PVA glue is added to the paint, this will give the vehicle a shinier finish and protect it a little.

Once made the vehicles can be tested on a flat surface, different surfaces and down a ramp to explore how they move and how to make them go faster, slower, further, etc.

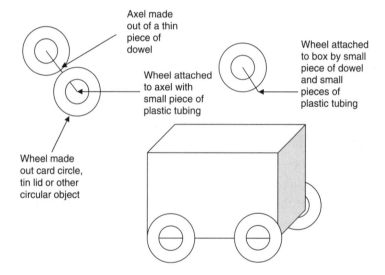

Figure 2.1 Fixing wheels to a box vehicle.

Reflection for early career professional

Try out the activity with your children.

- What support did you need to provide for children in your care?
- How could the activity of making a box-vehicle support development in other areas?
- What other design and make activities could you undertake in your class/ setting?

Reflection for leader/ manager

Try out the activity with different children in your setting. With your colleagues consider,

- How age and ability made a difference in the outcomes and success of the activity;
- How you could support different learners to maximize success;
- How else you could develop cross-curricular, design and make activities?

Photograph 2.2 Making a box model

Some issues in incorporating design and make activities in the early years

In this final section of the chapter, we will look at a few issues that need to be considered to ensure success in designing and making.

Creativity and relevance

In recent years much of the curriculum at Key stage 1 and in the Foundation Stage has become rather disconnected from everyday life and children often fail to see the relevance and purpose of what they are doing. Even if the designing and making stems from a fantasy or fictional activity, it may still be necessary for some explicit links to be made to the real world. It is important that professionals provide activities that are creative, relevant, child-centred and which encourage thinking skills, making learning *'an enjoyable and challenging experience'* (DfES 2003: 29). Problem solving activities can help to bridge the gap between the more passive activities suggested in some schemes of work and more vibrant teaching and learning experiences.

Practical activities and organization

Quality designing and making needs to be practical in order to develop understandings, skills and attitudes. This does pose some organizational problems for professionals as some practical design and make activities will need careful supervision and this may mean that a supporting adult needs to be available to 'keep an eye' on the children and to support when necessary. The adult will need to be well-briefed to allow the children to try things out, make mistakes and learn from those mistakes, but they also need to ensure that children are using tools safely and they also need to know how to do this. Practical problem solving tasks are best given to small groups. Sometimes a problem that one group has can be solved by the next group and in this way the children learn from each other. Children who are given ownership over their own learning and can make decisions about what they do and how they do it, who are allowed to make mistakes are more likely to be engaged and motivated and exhibit fewer behavioural problems. We also need to remember that ability is not easy to predict in designing and making and that children we regard as 'less able' may excel in more practical activities.

Covering the curriculum – quality or quantity?

Quality teaching and learning requires children in sustained thinking and problem-solving. This is not something that can be rushed. It can be argued that changing pupils' minds requires more than introducing them understandings and skills, but involves eliciting and using children's questions, ideas and thinking to guide learning experiences. It also involves accepting and encouraging their initiation of ideas, encouraging them in challenging each other's conceptualizations and ideas, and encouraging self-analysis and collection of real evidence to support ideas and reformulation of ideas in the light of new experience and evidence. This requires good conceptual and pedagogical understanding on the part of professionals in order to implement effective problem-solving and design and make strategies and to challenge children. The challenge is not only that effective learning comes from effective teaching and effective teaching requires knowledgeable adults, but also that quality learning needs quality time and this cannot be achieved in a curriculum that is over-full and when the main focus is a very narrow aspect of development in order to meet national targets in numeracy and literacy at Key Stage 1.

Focus on the learning objectives

Designing and making can support the achievement of learning objectives, although it is essential (as with any teaching) that objectives are clear and focused all throughout the teaching. A practical approach can support the achievement of learning objectives in a number of areas by providing important motivational factors which support learning. When children feel the topic is relevant and important they are more focused in their attention to detail and this has a powerful facilitative effect on cognitive functioning (see Shayer and Adey, 2002).

Recording – evidence for assessment?

Many professionals are concerned that they need records of the children's achievements for assessment purposes. In the early years professionals were good at using evidence from photographs, models and comments made by the children as evidence (QCA, 2003), but we must not devalue this as evidence as the children begin to be able to make marks on paper. All written recordings should only be undertaken if it will help to support the achievement of the learning objectives in design and making. Most practical design and make activities are often a good end in themselves and children who have to present and explain a model or solution to a problem are not only providing evidence of conceptual knowledge, but also of other recording skills such as recording in poster format, communicating findings to others and interpreting evidence.

References

Briggs, R. (1970) *Jim and the Beanstalk*. London: Penguin (Picture Puffin)

de Bóo M (2004) *The Curriculum Partnership: Early Years Handbook* Sheffield: Geography Association

DCSF, (2008) *The Early Years Foundation Stage; Setting the Standard for Learning, Development and Care for Children from Birth to Five; Practice Guidance.* London: DCSF

DfEE, (1999) *The National Curriculum: Handbook for Teachers in England.* London:DfEE/QCA

DfES (2003) *Excellence and Enjoyment. A Strategy for Primary Schools.* London: DfES

Green, M. (1978) *Mr Bembleman's Bakery.* New York: Parents Magazine Press

Hope, J. (2006) *Teaching Design and Technology at Key Stages 1 and 2.* Exeter: Learning Matters

Howe, A., Davies, D. and Richie, R. (2001) *Primary Design and Technology for the Future. Creativity, Culture and Citizenship.* London: David Fulton

Johnston, J. (2004) The Value of Exploration and Discovery, *Primary Science Review* 85: 21–23

Johnston, J. (2005) *Early Explorations in Science 2*nd *Edition* Maidenhead: Open University Press

Johnston, J. and Herridge, D. (2004) *Heinemann Explore Science for Reception.* Oxford: Heinemann

Johnston, J. and Nahmad-Williams, L. (2008) *Early Childhood Studies.* Harlow: Pearsons

Nichol, J. (2007) *Bringing the Steiner Waldorf Approach to your Early Years Practice.* London: David Fulton

QCA (2003) *Foundation Stage Profile.* London: QCA

Richie, R. (2001) *Primary Design and Technology.* London: David Fulton

Shayer, M. and Adey, P (eds) (2002) *Learning Intelligence. Cognitive Acceleration Across the Curriculum from 5 to 15 Years,* Buckingham: Open University Press

Siraj-Blatchford, J. and Siraj-Blatchford, I. (1998) Learning through making in the early years, in Smith, J. and Norman, E. (eds) *International Design and Technology Educational Research and Curriculum Development,* Loughborough University of Technology, 32–36

Siraj-Blatchford, J. and Siraj-Blatchford, I. (2001) Emergent Science and Technology in the Early Years. Paper presented at the 23rd *World Congress Of OMEP,* Santiago Chile July 31st to 4th August 2001

Siraj-Blatchford, J., and MacLeod-Brudenell, I. (1999) *Supporting Science, Design and Technology in the Early Years.* Buckingham: Open University Press

Sweet, B. (1996) Design and Technology – The Early Years in Whitebread, D. (ed.) (1996) *Teaching and Learning in the Early Years.* London: Routledge

Wilson, A. (2009) *Creativity in Primary Education 2nd Edition.* Exeter: Learning Matters

Information and Communication Technology

3

Chapter Outline

Introduction

More than ever before children are surrounded by technology. From an early age children can experience technology in a numerous ways inside and outside the home. Increasingly, technology is becoming part of the play experience of a child and therefore one of their cultural references. A range of technological play experiences can combine and accumulate for children and subsequently inform their early learning experiences.

Information and Communication Technology (ICT) has experienced an enormous and rapid change over the last few decades; it is now much more than a monitor, keyboard and computer. Understanding the potential of ICT and its diverse identity is useful when providing a range of opportunities. Indeed, it might be the non-traditional face of technology that could be more appropriate for use by children at a young age. In this chapter ICT will be discussed as technology in its broadest sense. Microphones, walkie talkies, metal detectors, sound amplifiers, bubble machines, remote control cars, floor robots and role play toys that use technology can all be placed in the category that is encompassed by ICT; it is this sort of technology that might bring the most useful experiences to children. Using technology like that listed above caters for a young child's desire and need to be active, move and explore, use their senses and their physicality. It is the creation of these types of learning opportunities that will be further explored.

This chapter also explores the issue of communication. The 'communication' aspect of ICT has often been the poor relation in the title ICT with emphasis being placed purely on the words information and technology. The Cambridge Review of the Primary Curriculum (Alexander and Flutter, 2009) demonstrates how the 'communication' aspect of ICT has been 'neglected' and argues that it should be reaffirmed in a wider definition of what can promote speaking and listening. This chapter seeks to address how a range of tools can be used to enrich and enhance the spoken language of children.

In the Early Years Foundation Stage (DCSF 2008) ICT is found in the section that studies Knowledge and Understanding of the World (KUW). The Early Learning Goals (DCSF 2008: 14, 15) stipulate that by the age of five children should:

- find out about and identify the uses of everyday technology and use information and communication technology and programmable toys to support their learning

Although ICT is situated within the KUW section of the document, I would argue that the best application of ICT is delivered as part of an integrated approach. ICT should occur as a natural addition to each of the six areas of learning in the Early Years Foundation Stage. In the course of the chapter several case studies seek to highlight how ICT can enhance all areas of the curriculum.

ICT for birth to 3 years of age

Very young infants and babies use their senses to explore the world. While the traditional notion of using a computer is certainly not applicable to the very young, many are actually exposed to a range of technology from an early age. Gadgets like battery operated mobiles or toys that may have lights and sound effects are often a child's first experience of technology. As babies become young infants they will explore a range of toys, some of which will make use of electronic effects. For example, playmates and playgyms, designed for very young infants, usually arrive equipped with buttons and pull down handles that might trigger flashing lights or tunes. As toddlers become young children it is likely that they will be surrounded by technology. For instance, if children watch TV programmes it is now likely that they will be directed to an accompanying interactive website.

While the growth and availability of electronic toys cannot be denied, there are those who point to associated dangers of using these sorts of play materials (Bronson, 1995, Palmer , 2006). Electronic toys and games can be viewed as 'bad' for the child and can be associated with all that is wrong with modern day childhood. Educationalists argue that children who are emerged into a quick paced, ever-changing technological world may subsequently suffer from a lack of creativity and short attention spans. For instance, the pitfalls of watching too much television from an early age have been widely debated. It is argued that television viewing can result in the formation of passive children who are reluctant to explore and interact. Proponents of a Steiner education argue that electronic technology should not in any way be in the young child's experience stating that this kind of play results in a feeling of emptiness and a demand for more, this is referred to a 'saturation entertainment' (Nicol, 2007). Palmer (2006) argues for the social limitations of young children who solitarily play with technology in their rooms suggesting that this can result in children becoming withdrawn. She also articulates the dangers of unsupervised children playing age–inappropriate computer games that have unsuitable content with the worry being that for children under 10 years old this sort of viewing could be emotionally destabilizing.

While there is not room in this text to comment further on the arguments referred to above, I would state that the 'way' technology is used with young children can result in some very creative learning opportunities. Electronic toys and games should be used amongst a range of other types of toys that stimulate their creativity and imagination. A child's interaction with ICT should be one that requires them to explore and discover. Some emerging texts are now advocating some of the benefits of using ICT in early childhood. Smith (2005) has observed a very young child interacting with a CD–ROM game and linked it to dramatic play, literacy development and learning processes. Siraj-Blatchford and Whitebread (2003) state that the appropriate use of technology can be a very active, social, intellectually stimulating and liberating experience for young children. These authors correctly point out that as with any resource, new technologies can be used well or badly.

Technology applied with an understanding of what makes for effective learning experiences for young children will result in good choices being made. Technology being used blindly as a time filler or to keep children occupied will naturally probably result in a poor experience. Types of technology, however, that advocate, via advertising and marketing, improvements for a young child's intelligence might be used with caution. Shops are awash with products that claim to 'strengthen' a child's brain power; some of these are technological devices. Lindon (2005: 127) urges that these products must be treated with care and that they make overblown claims. Products like this prey on concerned parents who are trying to give a child 'the best start in life' and never replace high quality interaction and stimulation provided by a trusted adult. These types of toys may require children to be involved in a learning situation that is too formal or didactic and may indeed limit creativity and exploration. Conversely, technology that is used wisely in conjunction with a range of other toys and with an adult who will interact and give the child their time could well bring about an effective experience.

Photograph 3.1 Playing with ICT in the early years (© Emma Jordan)

Case study

15-month-old Erin had a range of favourite toys. One was a bright, colourful, soft goldfish called Floss, a play shopping trolley was also dearly loved for its potential to collect a host of intriguing objects. One of her other favourite toys was one that required her to stack a range of colourful stars onto a supporting central pole. Once all stars were stacked this would trigger a series of lights to flash in a colourful fashion and cause one of about five prerecorded popular tunes to play. Erin quickly established a favourite tune she wished to trigger and this gave her the determination to refine her stacking skills in order that she could move and 'dance' to the resulting sounds. As Erin got older, when she came across and heard one of these popular tunes in her everyday activities she would always smile and say . . . 'I demember (remember) that toy that I can make flash when I pile up my stars'.

Reflection for early career professional

- When working with children note down all the toys that use technology. Are some more attractive to children than others? Why do you think this is?

Reflection for leader/manager

- Review some electronic toys available to children in your educational environment.
- Do these toys encourage explorative play? Can they be dropped, rolled, spun, squeezed and investigated or are children playing with them in a more limited fashion? What could you do to ensure that electronic toys can be used in a variety of ways to encourage exploration?

As the early learning goal states (referred to at the start of the chapter) young children should be made aware of how technology surrounds them and helps them in their everyday life and this can be started at a very early age. Day-to-day tasks in which children are involved can result in an immense amount of contact with technology and discussion about this can heighten a child's awareness.

Case study

Three-year-old Robin was baking with his childminder. They were making cup cakes. Robin had seen these cakes made on a television programme aimed at children and asked to make some. Robin's childminder downloaded the recipe from the programme's related website. With the help of an adult Robin found the required materials in the fridge and weighed out ingredients using scales that had a digital interface. When they added the fat to the mixture, they found it to be too hard, so they softened it using a microwave. The cake ingredients were mixed using an electric whisk and the cakes dished into containers, then baked in the oven. Robin helped his child minder to set the electric timer on the oven. While the cakes were baking Robin helped to clear up; they loaded the dishwasher and set it off on a wash cycle.

Reflection for early career professional

- Can you list all the instances the child in this case study interacts with technology?
- Take children on a walk and note all the instances of technology seen along your journey.
- Plan an activity with children where the everyday use of technology is highlighted to children.

Reflection for leader/manager

- What potential is there for children in your educational establishment to interact with and find out about the technology used in the daily life of the nursery, home, etc?

ICT for 3 to 5 years of age

This is the age when children are likely to come into contact with ICT in an educational setting, initially within a playgroup or nursery setting and then within the confines of a school experience in the Foundation Stage year. Children may enter an educational environment with a degree of sophisticated multimedia experiences; conversely some may have had very little contact with it. When entering an educational establishment the experience with technology should be acknowledged and the ICT on offer to the child should be in step with equipment that may be used in the home. Prensky (2005) has suggested the term 'digital native' for today's learners. These are people who have grown up with digital technology and who are fluent in the digital language of technology. This term is opposed to the 'digital immigrant' who has to gradually acclimatize themselves to technology and was not immersed in it from an early age. Educationalists should be committed to the role of technology and ensure that opportunities in school should not appear to be lacking or a poor relation to those on offer in the home. The recent *Independent Review of the Primary Curriculum* (Rose, 2009) discusses the importance of traditional methods of becoming literate but also refers to the fact that children should look at literacy in a broader sense. One of those being that they should be technologically literate and that a sound grasp of ICT is fundamental to engagement with society. The learning environment created in schools and nurseries should reflect this increasingly vital place of ICT.

ICT and play

When considering how children of this age should interact with ICT it is worth reviewing the general themes and principles of good practice set out in the Early Years Foundation Stage (EYFS) document (DCSF, 2008). Theme 3.3 'Enabling Environments' of the EYFS states that children need time to play with what interests them and that they should make heir own choices in their play objects. This is supported by the key message that spaces in which children learn should be:

- planned so that they can be used flexibly and an appropriate range of activities are provided.
- equipped with resources which are appropriate, well-maintained and accessible for all children.
- (a place where) young children thrive best in an environment that supports and promotes their active learning and development.

Theme 4.1. Learning and Development, and the accompanying commitments 'Play and Exploration' and 'Active Learning' are also of significance and worth detailing further.

- children need plenty of space and time to play, both outdoors and indoors.
- children who are allowed to play with resources and equipment before using them to solve a problem are more likely to solve the problem successfully.
- role-play areas allow children to take on and rehearse new and familiar roles.
- when children are actively involved in learning they gain a sense of satisfaction from their explorations and investigations.

Photograph 3.2 ICT in action

All the issues detailed in the list above are widely acknowledged and applied when it comes to access for children in many areas of the curriculum, but poor choices can be made when ICT is delivered. In a nursery ICT can be relegated to the idea of a child at a stand-alone computer. In schools there is a trend that either the youngest children get the oldest computers that are 'handed down' from higher key stages or that increasingly all computers are grouped together in an ICT suite; the children therefore only think they are accessing their time with technology during their visit to the suites. ICT suites are often unsuitable learning spaces for very young children. Frequently the height at which the equipment is placed is intended for older children and much time can be spent on logistical activities like entering over complex passwords during logging in. Taking a large group of young children into a suite is also very support intensive, requiring input from many adults who are often not available due to staffing problems; this results in children under utilizing their time and not making the most from software. By placing ICT access in a suite it is very difficult to apply the commitments and principles of good practice listed above. As Siraj-Blatchford and Siraj Blatchford (2003) note, ICT delivered in this format actively discourages the integration of technology with the rest of the curriculum. Children need to see ICT used in a meaningful context and for real purposes.

For young children ICT is much more than working on a computer; it should be made to be stimulating and motivating and should help children to creatively access the whole of the curriculum. Children should access technology in their learning just as they would access paint or use crayons to draw a picture. Technology should be an integrated part of a child's play not something that is seen as separate or special. An understanding of learning through play and discovery should be applied to the delivery of ICT. As Johnston (2004) advocates, children construct their own understanding through exploration and from the experience of discovery, as well as developing important skills and attitudes. Imaginative role-play that includes ICT-based resources provides a natural context for children to share play ideas and use products in creative ways. 'Hats are made from saucepans, cars from wooden blocks, princesses' cloaks from any material at hand. Such resources are important because they provide symbols for the children to play with' (Siraj-Blatchford & Siraj Blatchford 2003: 3). David (2003) urges for allowing sufficient time for play themes to develop and that providing open-ended resources allows children to stimulate innovative responses. As Poulter and Basford (2003) point out, when children are playing with ICT resources in this manner they take ownership of what they are doing and so are intrinsically motivated to learn. As a result of this, children will develop and reinforce new knowledge, skills and understanding. If a practitioner's view of ICT is that which occurs only on a computer in a suite, then the ideal previously detailed will not be realized. ICT should be offered through an integrated and playful approach.

Case study

Tooni is playing in the role play area. The topic for the class this term is the seaside. Tooni role plays a day out at the seaside. She dresses up in summer clothes and packs a bag full of equipment she might need for a day at the sea; sunglasses, sun cream, towel, hat, digital camera, portable CD player, play mobile phone and a bucket and spade. She plays in the sand area arranging small world play animals and making patterns with available shells and stones. She uses a metal detector to investigate the sand area further. She pretends to visit the shop to buy snacks and a fishing net. She withdraws money from the pretend ATM cash machine. She selects products for purchase in the shop and takes them to her friend, Harriet, at the check out. Her friend scans the products on the till and Tooni pays for the goods. Harriet then takes some pictures of Tooni in her dressing-up clothes. With the help of an adult Tooni is able to download and print out her picture. The picture is placed in a talking photo frame and put on display in the role play area. Tooni records a message on the photo frame so that when a button on the front of it is pressed she can hear her recorded description of her day out. Tooni recorded the phrase 'the sea sparkled in the sun'. Tooni also writes a talking postcard, she draws a picture of a shell, she writes some captions on the postcard, she records a spoken message and when triggered the card will play back her words.

Reflection for early career professional

- What curricular areas are accessed by the child described in this case study?
- How does this case study advocate speaking and listening?

Reflection for leader/manager

- If your children go into an ICT suite consider how you might make tasks meaningful and open ended.
- What ICT resources could be used for role play in your educational setting?

Practical task

- Look at the topics your children undertake, make links with ICT for all these topic areas – do any of the topics lend themselves to a role play corner that might include ICT? Make a plan that includes ICT in one role play scenario.

ICT and interaction

There is a pervasive and somewhat stereotypical view that ICT is an insular experience where people sit alone at a computer – the 'screen' replacing traditional forms of communication. This view needs to be revaluated; I would argue that ICT offers an entirely different set of learning opportunities. At present there is an emphasis on developing the spoken word in the classroom – this area of literacy has long been the poor relation in schools when compared to reading and writing which has tended to dominate the curriculum. Alexander (2004) calls for the potential for talk to be exploited in the classroom as an agent for not only social empowerment but also cognitive growth. Engaging children in a language-rich environment sounds relatively easy, however, actually producing successful, high-quality and enriching talk in a classroom can be challenging and requires a teacher who understands how to develop talk via a host of teaching strategies.

ICT does create scenarios where there are plenty of opportunities for talk. Spend time observing children undertaking well-planned, open-ended ICT activities and it is easy to see much discussion, questioning, collaboration, planning and compromise. Using a floor robot usually results in a discussion that involves all the attributes listed above. Higgins and Packard (2004) attribute this to the fact that many young children are enthusiastic about technology and this provides a focus for their talk. The best scenarios for learning with ICT provide opportunities for collaboration. Carefully chosen software (see below) or peripheral devices that promote open-ended tasks and an investigative approach will naturally result in discussion if two or more children are involved. For instance, observing children using a digital camera promotes a whole range of decisions. Conversation flows as to when to use it, why they should use it, how to operate it, how to get the best shot, evaluation of the picture and decisions as to whether to keep the picture. I have observed children aged 5 years using the movie facility on a digital camera with ease. Children who can be naturally quiet appear to be freed of inhibition when recording using a camera. The movie facility allows children to show their subject knowledge and understanding of a task and removes the burden of writing for the very young. On one occasion two children from a past class independently decided to make a movie of fossils that one of them had found while on holiday and had brought into class to show. The finished movie not only revealed much understanding of vocabulary associated with fossils, e.g. ammonites, belemnites, but also a good grasp of the processes involved in their formation. The description of the fossils also demanded the children to use an increasing range of vocabulary.

Along with peer-to-peer collaboration, ICT should be used in conjunction with adult facilitation. Leaving children alone on a computer or using a peripheral device will result in learning opportunities being ignored. For children to access Vygotsky's (1978) Zone of Proximal Development in order to progress their learning, an adult presence is required; this can often be ignored in relation to ICT-based activities. ICT can provide creative opportunities for talk, for instance children are usually eager to discuss with adults the meaning behind and reasons for pictures taken on a digital camera. Using a digital microscope is usually accompanied by a verbal description of what children can see. From initial whoops of delight and expressions of surprise microscope work can quickly be progressed so as to encourage children to articulate what they observe via the use of rich, descriptive language choices.

Photograph 3.3 Using a digital microscope

Software

Identified peripheral devices should be used for the delivery of worthwhile learning activities and their potential value must not be ignored. This is not to say, however, that some wisely selected PC-based activities are not also of importance. There are a wealth of programmes aimed at nursery and foundation stage children; some of these are free (e.g. many free programmes can now be downloaded from the internet) while some need to be purchased. Practitioners need an understanding of the numerous factors that combine to make one piece of software better than others. The more productive kind of software is that which is designed to cater for the usability issues of young children and those that adopt an open-ended approach. Software that is produced around the constructionist paradigm will offer many learning opportunities(Papert, 1993) will offer many learning opportunities. Software that requires children to think, question, problem solve, try out ideas and learn from mistakes is arguably much more productive than some software that will only accept one predetermined answer to a set question; this latter type of software is often referred to as 'drill and practise' software and is rather limited in its potential.

An excellent and freely downloadable application can be found at *www.poissonrouge.com*. This piece of software offers more learning opportunities than some commercially-marketed programs. Poisson Rouge covers all areas of learning and offers excellent usability to nursery and foundation stage children. All of this huge application can be accessed without having to have a great reading ability. The software can be navigated via the use of pictures and icons and this removes many of the textual barriers that can often be associated with software aimed at young children. Poisson Rouge advocates a truly explorative approach designed around constructivist principles. Children who use this application are required to experiment and enquire. They are encouraged to ask questions like 'what happens if I click on this?' 'How do I stop this?' 'Let's try and fit all these pieces together'. This kind of learning environment will encourage children to play for a sustained period and is a far more beneficial learning experience than an application that 'tests' children on spelling or number recognition and will only allow them to progress through the application if they submit one predetermined answer with no chance of variation of enquiry.

Practical task

Go to poission rouge.com and investigate the tasks provided in this program. Compare this program's excellent design principles to other pieces of software you have in your educational establishment. How might you incorporate this program into the learning opportunities provided in your educational establishment?

Control technology

The ICT Early Learning Goal specifies that children should experience working with programmable toys. Using programmable toys are a child's initial experience of learning how to use technology to '*make things happen*' and acts as a precursor to the similarly named theme detailed in the National Curriculum ICT Programme of Study (DFEE, 1999). Using technology 'to make things happen' is also commonly known as control technology. Control technology is often misunderstood by teachers and can be associated with feelings of under confidence and challenge when delivering this subject area (Duffty, 2006). Put simply, control involves the application of an instruction, or series of instructions, in order to operate a device. This area of learning evolves in to more complex tasks that ultimately culminate in children being able to program a computer that in turn controls equipment. This area of the curriculum is of utmost importance for two reasons.

Examples of control technology are all around in modern life. Fridge temperature control mechanisms, traffic light operation, street lights turning on and off, doors opening automatically all use control technology to function; it is important that young children are aware of the importance of these mechanisms and have opportunities to identify and discuss them.

Control technology is a very powerful way to promote thinking skills and an investigative approach. Well-planned control lessons will require children to articulate their thought processes in a logical way. They will experience learning through an approach that requires them to use trial and error, learn from their mistakes, ask questions like 'what happens if . . . ' and systemically record sequenced instructions. Well-planned control lessons can be very engaging and result in children sustaining their concentration in order to successfully complete a task. Through very simple beginnings in nursery and the foundation stage, this sort of learning situation can eventually be associated with the development of higher order thinking skills such as application, analysis and synthesis as identified by Bloom et al (1956) in his taxonomy of learning.

Case study

In a nursery 3-year-old Susie was playing with a remote control caterpillar. The controller she was using had one button on it which, if manipulated appropriately, she could use to move the toy forwards or backwards. She used controller to move the caterpillar from leaf to leaf so that she could 'feed' an insect. Four-year-old Kate also attended the same nursery, in the outdoor area she had built a play car park out of large wooden blocks and was also using a remote control car in order to park the car in the car park. To do this task she had to use her remote control to turn right and left to move around the car park. Kate had to have a steady grip of the controller so as to keep the car moving in a straight line and negotiate it into the parking space using her reverse and forward functions. Her friend, Max was also using a remote car to park his car and they were having a race to see who could park first.

Reflection for early career professional

- One of the problems found in the delivery of control in educational settings is that there is confusion in the pitching of learning experiences and ensuring that activities have a sense of progression. These different tasks have two clear levels of challenge, but can you think of others that could be set as introductory activities of this nature.
- What do you think is the next level of complexity in this area of learning?
- What other skills, not just ICT, are children developing when undertaking these activities.

Reflection for leader/manager

- Think about the different devices you have available in your educational setting that allow children to undertake control activities.
- In what way do your control devices allow for adequate progression of learning?
- What organizational and resourcing issues need to be addressed when using programmable devices?

Transition to Key Stage 1 (5 to 7 years of age)

As children reach Key Stage 1 they will follow the National Curriculum Programme of Study for ICT (DFEE, 1999). ICT is now formalized into a separate subject area instead of being one of a number of subjects under the title of Knowledge and Understanding of the World. As well as detailing ICT in its own subject area, each curriculum subject PoS makes demands for the use of ICT; this can lead to a tension as to how ICT should be delivered.

ICT – discrete subject or cross-curricular tool?

A question I am often asked by both pre-service and qualified teachers involves concerns as to whether ICT should be taught as a discrete subject or if it should be accessed as an enhancing element of each area of the curriculum. Put simply, ICT should be taught both discretely and across the curriculum. The most effective ICT in Key Stage 1 should be integrated appropriately into the curriculum just as it is in the Foundation Stage (O'Hara, 2004; Rose, 2009). ICT is only meaningful if it is delivered in context and used for realistic and useful purposes through cross-curricular subjects. Increasingly government reports (Alexander and Flutter, 2008; Rose, 2009) call for a dovetailing of the EYFS (2008) and the National Curriculum (1999) in order to make the transition between these two stages less problematic. The good practices of an integrated, playful, approach as detailed by the Early Years Foundation Stage document (2008) are being increasingly utilized in Key Stage 1. As children use more complex ICT techniques in Key Stage 1, this embedded and engrained use of ICT can, however, only be realized if children have learnt some basic skills and this is where some discrete subject teaching is appropriate.

ICT skills

Children do need to be taught some simple skills and techniques. Routine functions like cutting, copying and pasting, selecting a picture to insert into a document or conducting a basic internet search might require some initial instruction that could form part of a discrete and dedicated ICT lesson.

ICT capability

Learning the techniques described above are not really very difficult. But combining a number of techniques and knowing when to use them is much more sophisticated. The best and more advanced sort of ICT occurs when children use it as a tool for learning. Children should apply their knowledge of ICT in order to solve problems and enhance their learning when accessing other curriculum areas. Children would have to use many problem-solving skills when creating simple animations of a story, for instance. Children need to learn when to recognize that the use of ICT might be appropriate and use their skills accordingly in a variety of contextualized situations. Potter and Darbyshire (2005) call this type of effective ICT – 'ICT capability' and these authors argue that it is this type of ICT that encourages conceptual understanding and makes use of higher order skills. Potter and Darbyshire (2005) state that capability cannot occur without due recognition and time given to development of skills; teachers should have a good understanding of ICT to ensure the two occur and to avoid the limiting effect of teaching skills alone. The case studies listed below exemplify an integrated cross-curricular application of ICT that reveal a child's capability.

Case studies

Year 1 were studying the traditional tale of the three little pigs. The children had been particularly focused on recalling the sequence of the story. The class were also studying positional language in numeracy; the teacher used ICT to make a link between these. The teacher used a transparent mat on which she drew a grid of 10 cm by 10 cm squares. She then cut up pictures of the story and laminated them. She asked a group of children to place the pictures in the correct sequence under the grid. Using a programmable device (e.g. a Beebot) the children instructed the floor robot to move to the pictures in the correct order so as to demonstrate their understanding of the story.

Shelley was asked to write a recount of her recent trip to an animal park. She was having trouble getting started on her writing. With a friend she decided to see if she could access the park's accompanying website. She first 'googled' the name of the

⇨

Case studies—Cont'd

park (with adult supervision) in order to access the site. She then navigated around the site clicking on hotspots that caught her interest. She was reminded of the fact that she saw an eagle owl. She also saw pictures of a tarantula and a scorpion and said 'oh yes . . . spiders and scorpions are venomous . . . '. Shelley remembered how she had watched ants running along a rope carrying leaves on their back. Shelley also talked about the fact that they went to the play area before they went home on the bus. She printed out a picture of a butterfly and tarantula to add to her work.

Reflection for early career professional

- What areas of the curriculum are accessed by the two case studies described above?
- How are the children using their ICT capability in the scenarios, what skills and routines would the children have to learn in order to access the activities?

Reflection for leader/manager

- Consider if your staff understand the difference between ICT skills and capability?

Practical task

- Design a task that enhances your current unit of work that requires children to use their ICT capability.

Conclusion

ICT changes and develops rapidly and this can make it a difficult curriculum area to keep abreast of. ICT is now much more than a computer and keyboard – a wealth of peripheral devices can be used to adopt an active mode of delivery. ICT should be delivered via a playful approach. Integrated and contextualized ICT activities that require children to construct and apply their knowledge make for the most worthwhile learning opportunities. ICT should be carried out in collaboration with adults or other children and can promote rich opportunities for the development of talk. ICT is a very engaging medium that many children find motivating. Good subject knowledge of ICT, awareness of current developments and understanding of pedagogy is key to creating an environment that provides opportunities that progress learning.

References

Alexander, R. J. (2004) *Towards Dialogic Teaching: Rethinking Classroom Talk.* New York: Dialogos

Alexander, R. J. and Flutter, J. (2009) *Towards a New Primary Curriculum: a Report from the Cambridge Primary Review: Past and Present.* Cambridge: University of Cambridge Faculty of Education

Bloom, B., Krathwohl, D., Engelhart, D., Furst, E. and Hill, W. (1956) *Taxonomy of Educational Objectives: Cognitive Domain.* London: Longman

Bronson, B. (1995) *The Right Stuff for Children Birth to Eight: Selecting Play Materials to Support Development.* Washington: National Association for the Education of Young Children

David, T. (2003). What do we know about teaching young children?. Available from: http://www. standards.dfes.gov.uk/eyfs/resources/downloads/eyyrsp1.pdf [3 May, 2009]

DCSF (2008) *Practice Guidance for the Early Years Foundation Stage: Setting the Standards for Learning, Development and Care for Children from Birth to Five.* London: Department for Children, Schools and Families

DCSF (2008) *Statutory Framework for the Early Years Foundation Stage.* London: Department for Children, Schools and Families

DFEE (1999) *The National Curriculum.* London: Crown Copyright and QCA

DfES (2007) *The Early Years Foundation Stage: Setting the Standard for Learning, Development and Care for Children from Birth to Five; Practice Guidance.* London: Department for Education and Skills

Duffty, J. (2006) *Extending Knowledge in Practice.* Exeter: Learning Matters

Higgins, S., and Packard, N. (2004) *Meeting the Standards in Primary ICT: A Guide to the ITT NC.* London: Routledge Falmer

Johnston, J. (2004). The Value of Exploration and Discovery. *Primary Science Review.* 85, 21–23

Lindon, J. (2005) *Understanding Child Development. Linking Theory and Practice.* Abbingdon: Hodder Arnold

Nicol, J. (2007) *Bringing the Steiner Waldorf Approach to Your Early Years Practice.* London: Routledge.

O'Hara, M. (2004) *Teaching 3–8.* London: Continuum

Palmer, S. (2006) *Toxic Childhood. How the Modern World is Damaging Our Children and What We Can Do about it.* Orion: London

Papert, S. (1993) *Mindstorms: Children, Computers and Powerful Ideas. 2nd Edition* Hemel Hempstead: Harvester Wheatsheaf

Potter, F. and Darbyshire, C. (2005) *Understanding and Teaching the ICT National Curriculum.* London: David Fulton Publishers

Poulter, T., and Basford, J. (2003) *Using ICT in Foundation Stage Teaching.* Exeter: Learning Matters

Prensky, M. (2005). *Learning in the Digital Age, Educational Leadership.* 63(4), 8–13

Rose, J. (2008) The Independent Review of the Primary Curriculum: Interim Report. Available: http:// publications. teachernet.gov.uk (accessed April 2009)

Rose, J. (2009) Independent Review of the Primary Curriculum: Final Report. Available: http://publications.teachernet.gov.uk (accessed May 2009)

Siraj-Bltachfored, I., and Siraj-Bltachford, J. (2003) *More than Computers: Information and Communication Technology in the Early Years.* London: The British Association for Early Childhood

Siraj-Blatchford, I., and Whitebread, D. (2003) *Supporting Information and Commuinications Technology in the Early Years.* Berkshire: Open University Press

Smith, C. (2005) The CD-ROM Game in Marsh, J. (ed.) *Popular Culture, New Media and Digital Literacy in Early Childhood.* Oxford: RoutledgeFalmer

Vygotsky, L. (1978) *Mind in Society.* London and Cambridge, MA: Harvard University Press

4

Chapter Outline

Introduction

I can vividly recall how my interest in history occurred. There were no fireworks, no great teaching moments, no revolutionary lessons; it was merely the historical textbooks we were given in primary school. The pictures held my attention, I was fascinated by the strange looking clothes the grand ladies and gentlemen wore. I would gaze at the timber-framed houses we learnt about. The pictures were so colourful and so different from the world I knew. Although we learnt about 'kings and queens' I also liked finding out about the lives of children, what they played with, what they studied at school, I was fascinated and somewhat disbelieving to know that indeed some children never went to school in their whole lives, they could not read or write and had to sign their names with a cross.

The arguments for the place of history in the school timetable, what should be taught, when it should be taught and how it should be delivered are long and lengthy and they will be explored in more detail during the course of this chapter. However, the above paragraph, although portraying a rather stereotypical view of the subject, I think, articulates precisely why history holds such an important place in the curriculum; history is interesting and captures the imagination and sense of curiosity. As a child I felt it was simply wonderful to spend time on a lesson finding out about the past, I relished the opportunity to spend time drawing the colourful characters we learnt about, ensuring I applied attention to detail to my pictures – Tudor framed houses being my particular expertise to my young eye. Without these lessons to which I so looked forward, my time at school would have been a poorer place. A curriculum without references to the past and all that this brings would be a more sterile and less creative environment. Indeed, this attention given early in my school years resulted in a much anticipated interest in secondary school and eventual degree and life-long interest in the subject.

The discipline of history and the actual work of historians will be examined more closely in the section of the chapter that focuses on children in Key Stage 1. Here distinctive forms of enquiry and investigation will be explored more fully in its relation and application to children of this age. At this point it is worthwhile spending a little time outlining two other very important themes that historical awareness brings to a child which I view as crucial to the curriculum as a whole. Apart from creativity and imagination, history brings with it an ability to empathize. Wood and Holden (1995) call this 'the ability to stand in someone else's shoes' and to try and understand why people behaved as they did'. To empathize with a different perspective and to appreciate different points of view has positive consequences right across the curriculum and enters the realm of social and emotional development. Moreover, historical thinking requires children to understand about their identity, where they came from, how they fit into the place where they live and who came before them; this might be within a very young child's own living memory or it might be taking a longer perspective for a more mature youth. This eventually blossoms into a child being able to make cultural references about how their lives relate to others, again a theme that has far reaching benefits that stretch beyond the realms of history teaching. These factors alone make a compelling case for the role of history within the curriculum.

Much of this chapter is dedicated to pre-National Curriculum (DFEE & QCA, 1999) history and takes its lead from the detail identified in the *Practice Guidance for the Early Years Foundation Stage* (DCSF, 2008). While the importance of creativity, empathy and cultural identity have already been described, it might seem that history as a subject is a troublesome concept when applied to young children. Anecdotal evidence from pre-service teachers reveals that they feel teaching history to very young children before Key Stage 1 would initially seem a rather difficult prospect. The past could appear to be remote and challenging to access. Indeed, for young children it would be somewhat pointless for them to be learning about historical facts, times and dates. O'Hara and O'Hara (2001) describe the traditional teaching of historical content to very young children as 'wholly inappropriate' and one which would clash with the 'holistic view of the world that young children are thought to adopt'. This thought is echoed by Wood and Holden (1995) who state that many teachers have questioned the relevance of history in the early years and doubt children's capabilities to engage with seemingly abstract concepts. While I would agree with the above sentiments, it could be argued that children can be meaningfully involved in a range of 'starter' activities that will prepare them for what will eventually become a more recognizable history lesson. While historical approaches with young children need to be thought through carefully, there is an important place for the emergence of this subject area, much of this chapter will concentrate on identifying this development.

Time from birth to 3 years of age

Historical understanding for this age group is inextricably linked to the development of the child as a whole. The *Practice Guidance for the Early Years Foundation Stage* (DCSF, 2008) suggests the following:

Birth–11 months
  Anticipate repeated sounds, sights and actions
8–20 months
  Get to know and enjoy daily routines, such as getting-up time, mealtimes, nappy time, and bedtime
16–26 months
  Begin to understand that things might happen 'now'
  Associate a sequence of actions with daily routines
22–36 months
  Anticipate specific time-based events such as mealtimes or home time
  Understand some talk about immediate past and future, for example, 'before', 'later' or 'soon'

These recommendations could easily be applied to the common sense rules of raising a small child and as detailed in the previous section for some it might be hard to associate these statements with the traditional notion of 'history'. It does, however, create the very beginnings of an awareness of skills that can be linked to processes that are then developed in the pre-school and the foundation stage.

Time from 3 to 5 years of age

During this age phase most children will be carrying out their educational experience within a nursery, play school or more formal Foundation Stage setting. At this stage of learning, history is not detailed in a discrete subject area in the *Practice Guidance for the Early Years Foundation Stage* (DCSF, 2008), but can be found detailed under the general heading of Knowledge and Understanding of the World. In the area of '*Learning and Development*' the statements that are associated with history are grouped together under the title of '*Time*' and are specified as follows:

- Begin to differentiate between past and present
- Understand about the seasons of the year and their regularity
- Use time-related words in conversation.
- Make short-term future plans

The associated Early Learning Goal that can be found in the *Statutory Framework for the Early Years Foundation Stage* (DCSF, 2007) is phrased:

- Find out about past and present events in their own lives, and in those of their families and other people they know

The skills and ideas associated with time that will be discussed further in this section of the chapter can be linked to many other areas of the curriculum. Much of what is discussed in relation to developing sequencing skills has numerous links to mathematical thinking. The links to literacy are unavoidable and a discussion on the passing of time has direct benefits for speaking and listening and the development of a more complex vocabulary. Furthermore activities like sequencing stories and creating recounts are usually associated with literacy but also help with the development of an understanding of the passing of time. The fact that many of the activities are deeply cross-curricular are indicative of the nature of the Early Years Foundation Stage document (DCSF, 2008) and enhance the 'whole child' approach of cognitive, social and emotional development at this stage. The practitioner, does however, need to have a firm grasp on historical processes so he/she can identify and assess the development of historical understanding. It is often common and perfectly understandable to confuse objectives for lessons. What needs to be avoided is the identification of 'history' skills as an objective when in actual fact the main thrust of the lesson is literacy based but uses a historical theme via which it is taught. This can result in children who have learnt historical facts (which might quickly be forgotten) but little else. A practitioner needs to understand historical processes in order to give the best sort of learning opportunities and to be able to make appropriate assessments of a child's capabilities in this area.

The development of an understanding of time

Most of the phrases about historical learning in the *Practice Guidance for the Early Years Foundation Stage* (DCSF, 2008) as listed above, relate to the development of the passing of time and the eventual understanding of chronology. Wood and Holden (1995) state that although we tend to think of history in terms of periods and centuries, young children need to learn the initial basic language of smaller periods of time in order to be able to frame their understanding of the past at a later stage in their cognitive growth. I like to think of this as setting in place important 'building blocks' and laying firm foundations for future historical understanding. It would be irrelevant and meaningless for children to use advanced historical language but it is of great value to begin this concept of time by using more pedestrian terms like today, tomorrow, last weekend, next week and even phrases like next month or 'at Christmas time' and 'in the summer', etc.

An understanding of time usually begins in the home between a child and his/her parents. The importance of dialogue and conversing fully with the child in order to help develop a sense of time is very important. Below is a simple conversation that parents usually have countless times with their children. It is the patient repetition and reinforcement of this sort of conversation that will gradually result in an understanding of the passing of time.

> Child: When do we go to play with Sam?
> Parent: At 10 'o' clock tomorrow morning.

Child: *How far away is that from now, how many sleeps is that?*
Parent: *One more night, the sun will go down, it will get dark.*
Child: *Does that mean we have to have dinner before we go?*
Parent: *Yes, and we will have breakfast tomorrow morning too.*
Child: *I can't wait, do you think we will be able to take the dog for a walk?
          What is the time now, is it dinner time? What time is dinner? Do we have
          enough time to go and see the ducks before dinner?*

An early development of chronology is also developed within nursery and foundation stage classes. Anecdotal evidence has demonstrated that children usually arrive at school using a vocabulary relating to the passing of time but often it is used incorrectly. Children need to use the past tense correctly. When I had just qualified as a teacher it took me a long time, and many confusing conversations, to realize that children often use terms like tomorrow and yesterday incorrectly and actually get them the wrong way around. It can take a long time to correct this. Simple and common sense practice can rectify this by constant reminders of asking what the children did yesterday or telling the class what is happening tomorrow. It is the use of these phrases in different contexts by the practitioner and careful appreciation of the spoken word of the child that will eventually determine the correct use of a time-related vocabulary.

Children need to learn to frame time periods by learning about their own lives and change within it. Cooper (2007) points out that a staple of early years practice has been to talk about changes in a child's life and the implications of this. While this may not be called historical exploration, the passing of time is ingrained in the foundation stage curriculum and marks the beginning of this type of historical process. Children gain much by trying to conduct sequencing activities like correctly ordering pictures of themselves and then trying to guess what age they might be in each photograph. Asking the children to address activities like classifying different size clothes into correct age phases provokes much thinking and places a demand on them to sequence artefacts. I can remember the year that I asked young children to bring in photographs of themselves as babies, the photographs were placed on a wall and then the children were asked to discuss which photo belonged to each child. The resulting discussion was lengthy and an excellent starter for the children to begin making reasoned guesses as to which photo belonged to whom and why. The conversation was extended by trying to guess the identity of parents and siblings who might also be in the photos. The satisfying nature of this activity was that the conversation did not last for just one session but was returned to over and again during the course of weeks the pictures remained on display. The fact that they were placed at the entrance of my classroom where parents would congregate also involved many other adults in valuable, incidental discussions of the pictures that involved the children. It is sometimes those incidental, spontaneous conversations which are so important in making children feel special and unique and can add to their exploration of their sense of self.

Learning about the past from the extended community

The Early Learning Goal for Time (DCSF, 2008) states that children should not only learn about their own lives but also about the lives of people around them. Extended families and communities can provide a wealth of potential investigation for children that can be tapped into by schools and nurseries. Listening to stories about past, events told by grandparents and other older adults can act as useful discussion starters and act as a stimulus for children raising questions and initiating curiosity in the past. Hoodless (2008) discusses the value of using family connections not just in relation to historical understanding but in the dual capacity of helping children to recognize their own unique qualities, she links this to effective learning techniques as recognized in the *Practice Guidance for the Early Years Foundation Stage* (DCFS, 2008). Hoodless (2008) also acknowledges the importance of providing *opportunities* to understand time which should involve parents and the local neighbourhood. There should also be opportunities presented in the indoor and outdoor learning environment where children can re-enact their family experiences via role play.

Case study

Four-year-old Robert had recently accidentally injured his arm which resulted in him spending time in hospital, he had to have his arm in plaster. When he had returned home he spent time with his grandmother who looked after him while his mum went out to work. Talking about his time in hospital caused his grandmother to recall and discuss a protracted period of time she spent in hospital as a child due to

Case study—Cont'd

operations on the poorly developed bones in her foot. She and Robert talked about how their experiences in hospital were similar and different. Robert's grandmother talked about how she had not been allowed home and had to stay on a ward due to an outbreak of diphtheria in the area. She recounted how she had attended hospital school and how her parents could only visit for certain times of the day; this differed from Robert's experiences when his mother had stayed in hospital overnight with him. The best part of the story was when Robert's granny described when it had snowed while in hospital and all the children had been wheeled outside so that they could have a snowball fight while still remaining in bed.

On his return to school, Robert's teacher invited his granny into school so that she could share her story with all of the children. The story proved fascinating to the children and provoked many questions, especially the part about the snowball fight. Robert's grandmother brought in photographs of her time as a child, the children spent time trying to correctly identify Robert's grandmother. Other photographs that were brought in showed Robert's grandmother as a young woman which some children identified as Robert's mother due to family likeness. This led to a whole series of questions like 'who is the oldest, Robert's mum or Robert's granny?' and 'why are there no pictures of Robert's granny's mum and dad?'

Reflection for early career professional

- Think about how you can use parents and extended families in your setting in order to find out about the past.
- This encounter provided many opportunities to discuss the past; do you give your children enough starting points through which the past can be accessed?

Reflection for leader/manager

- How could this learning opportunity be extended, how might you progress the historical thinking in this situation?

The use of story

The use of story in aiding the development of historical understanding cannot be ignored. Story helps children make sense of the world around them in all aspects of the curriculum not just historical understanding. Stories like *Owl Babies* (Waddell & Benson, 1992) and the *Very Hungry Caterpillar* (Carle,

2002) can be used to enhance numerous curriculum areas but in a historical sense they can be utilized to help children understand the concept of the passing time in simple terms like night and day and yesterday and tomorrow. Stories under the genre of myths and legends and fairy tales, although not based in historical fact, do importantly introduce children to skills like connecting cause and effect that can be expanded in later school years. Cox and Hughes (1998) explore the link between fiction and historical understanding in some detail. They stress that amongst others, stories can act as a vehicle for historical understanding; the internal chronology and narrative form of a story provide children with support to order and recount the past. These authors also argue that through exploring the beliefs and actions of characters in stories children can begin to appreciate the feelings and motivations of people and important historical process. Low-Beer and Blyth (1990) agree with these arguments adding that storytelling can often be neglected in favour of historical activities such as learning from evidence and artefacts which may be seen as more important in educational settings. These authors link storytelling and the development of role-playing stating that children initiated early into the excitement of the past by good storytelling will naturally want to start role-playing if encouraged by their teachers. Role-playing can be a good way to check to see if a child has understood the content and meaning of a story.

Photograph 4.1 Re-telling the story of the hungry caterpillar (© Emma Jordan)

Transition to Key Stage 1 (5 to 7 years of age)

As children leave the cross-curricular approach of the foundation stage, they move onto study history as a discrete subject as detailed in the National Curriculum (DFEE & QCA, 1999). The Programme of Study for History at Key Stage 1 currently stands as follows:

Knowledge, Skills and Understanding

Chronological understanding

1 Pupils should be taught to:
  1 place events and objects in chronological order
  2 use common words and phrases relating to the passing of time [for example, before, after, a long time ago, past].

Knowledge and understanding of events, people and changes in the past

2 Pupils should be taught to:
  1 recognize why people did things, why events happened and what happened as a result
  2 identify differences between ways of life at different times.

Historical interpretation

3 Pupils should be taught to identify different ways in which the past is represented.

Historical enquiry

4 Pupils should be taught:
  1 how to find out about the past from a range of sources of information [for example, stories, eye-witness accounts, pictures and photographs, artefacts, historic buildings and visits to museums, galleries and sites, the use of ICT-based sources]
  2 to ask and answer questions about the past

Organization and communication

5 Pupils should be taught to select from their knowledge of history and communicate it in a variety of ways [for example, talking, writing, using ICT]

The above programme of study is taught via a range of historical themes which are listed under the term 'Breadth of Study'. The breadth of study for Key Stage 1 is currently specified as:

a   changes in their own lives and the way of life of their family or others around them

b   the way of life of people in the more distant past who lived in the local area or elsewhere in Britain

c   the lives of significant men, women and children drawn from the history of Britain and the wider world [for example, artists, engineers, explorers, inventors, pioneers, rulers, saints, scientists]

d   past events from the history of Britain and the wider world [for example, events such as the Gunpowder Plot, the Olympic Games, other events that are commemorated].

O'Hara and O'Hara (2001) discuss some of the background to the National Curriculum (DFEE & QCA, 1999) and reveal how the Programme of Study came into being. During the formation of the history curriculum fierce debate took place over what should be included. Some historians argued for content while others argued for the importance of skills and processes where the historical content was largely irrelevant and just the medium through which all important skills were taught. What resulted was a compromise and a large curriculum that detailed the need for both content and skills. The five skilled elements that comprise the 'Knowledge Skills and Understanding' part of the curriculum are taught through the content listed in the section entitled 'breadth of study.'

At this time of writing, the curriculum is in a state of flux and possible transition; it is the subject of intense scrutiny and political debate. Rose (2009) in his *Independent Review of the Primary Curriculum: Final Report*, proposes a new curriculum that places subjects into six broad areas of learning. History is placed alongside other subjects into an area of learning called Historical, Geographical and Social Understanding. The curriculum as proposed by Rose (2009) advocates a cross-curricular approach similar to the established good practice found in the Early Years Foundation Stage document (DCSF, 2008). Rose (2009) argues that this approach allows for the continued integrity of subjects but lessens the rigidity of boundaries encouraging children and teachers to think creatively. It could be feared that individual subjects will suffer from the loss of subject identity if this curriculum becomes statutory and is likely to re-inflame the debate of the poor status of humanities in the curriculum in comparison to 'core curriculum' subjects. In the case of history, however, the Historical Association currently takes a stance in favour of the proposed new curriculum stating:

> that the National Curriculum as it stands is over prescribed, and this is detrimental to teaching and learning. We fully support a modified framework that supports the development of a less prescriptive and a more flexible National Curriculum that draws upon subjects like history as tools for learning, as indicated in the report. (Rose, 2009: 15)

If change in the curriculum does occur in the near future and history becomes associated with other humanities subjects, as with the foundation stage, the practitioner must have an excellent understanding of historical processes in order to be able to fully identify their use and application by children so that they do not become lost and confused with other subjects. The rest of this chapter will therefore briefly explore some of the five key skills from the 'Knowledge, Skills and Understanding' History Programme of Study for Key Stage 1 in the National Curriculum (DFEE & QCA, 1999).

The development of chronological understanding

Children in Key Stage1 need to continue to develop their chronological under-standing by learning to sequence objects and events and use language associ-ated with the passing of time. Children apply their chronological knowledge not only to their own lives and that of family but also extending to people in the distant past. Teaching chronology to young children is a complex business and inextricably entwined with a child's development in other curricular sub-jects as explained earlier in this chapter. Cooper (2002) states that children in Key Stage 1 build up a chronological understanding in a piecemeal way and that it is a broadening rather than a hierarchical process. She argues that chil-dren gradually build up a map of the past that is constantly changing as new information is added. She reasons against teaching a chronological framework that becomes merely a rehearsal of a set of basic, meaningless dates that will be hard to remember stating that children need to be equipped with *causes* for change so that chronological information is given depth and substance. O'Hara and O'Hara (2001) state as children get older they are better able to compare their own lives with that of children in the past and maybe able to manage to sequence two or three events from a different historical period. These authors state that while their comprehension maybe limited it would be unlikely to improve if children are denied *opportunities* to extend and enhance their learning about the past. I would agree with these authors, it could be argued that while learning about different time periods maybe challenging, the discussion and opportunities that are given gradually build up a child's 'sense of time' where eventual connections between time periods are made during the later primary phase. Chronology should be introduced as an accompaniment to a broad investigation into one time period; the didactic rehearsal of empty facts should be avoided.

The difficulties of establishing a chronological awareness are exemplified in the case study detailed below.

Case study: Developing chronological awareness

Year 1 Issie was learning about the history of the village where she lived. She was recounting the story of the origins of the village to a teaching assistant. She demonstrated that she had remembered details of the story very well. She discussed how the village had developed as a tourist destination due to the discovery of water enriched by minerals. She recounted how the water had been discovered by a farmer and his herd of cows; drinking the water appeared to make the herd healthier. Issie described how as people got to know about the 'special water' lots of homes and shops were 'set up' and that even some hotels appeared. Issie finished her recount by stating that after all this had happened God then made humans to live in the village.

Reflection for early career professional

- This recount shows how children can often get chronology confused and find it difficult to connect up periods of time. How might you go about correcting this child's misconception about time?

Reflection for leader/manager

- Do your staff understand the complexities about teaching chronological understanding? How might this theme be tackled using a cross-curricular approach?

The use of ICT can often be a useful aid when addressing the challenges presented by chronological understanding. I can recall the first, very powerful experience of being shown the use of an interactive whiteboard. It was used to show the chronological sequence of the Tudor monarchs. The colour given by the board brought a seemingly distant past to life via the graphical representation of the different monarchs. What was more noticeable, however, was the ease with which these graphics could be moved to be placed in order alongside pictures of significant events from the period. The overall impression given was a release from the tedium of placing dates on a timeline to be replaced with a broader and deeper learning experience that took the form of a discussion of how and why people and places were sequenced and interconnected. While the description of this whiteboard activity might be more suited to Key Stage 2 children, the board is a useful tool for similar and simpler chronological activities. For example, the board can be used for showing photographs of different times of the school day which can then be manipulated and reordered by young children or sequencing pictures of special events in the school that have taken place over the past year.

Knowledge and understanding of events, people and changes in the past

This skill is concerned with helping children understand about people and events in the past. Children need to appreciate similarities and differences between past and present and start to investigate why people might have acted in a certain way. This key skill might be perhaps considered a more accessible area of learning for young children than some of the other key elements as it does involve some use of factual knowledge. With young children an active learning approach might be best employed for them to begin to understand the past in a meaningful and memorable way. For instance, it is currently a popular choice for schools to hold a 'Victorian' or a 'Tudor' day. Here children come to school dressed as a person from a set historical period and spend the day in that role. For instance, during a Tudor day a child might explore differences in the clothes worn during that time period, they might cook some receipes using ingredients only available in Tudor times, they might take part in Tudor dances in order to find out about social custom in Tudor times. While learning the dances the children will be listening to Tudor music and learning about the instruments that were used in the past. By experiencing history in this manner children might begin to progress their learning from just using factual knowledge to, more importantly, understanding the reasons why or how people acted in certain ways. For instance, dressing in the manner of a Tudor person and trying to carryout a Tudor dance wearing the heavy clothes worn by members of the upper classes, will make children appreciate how restricting it was to move under so many layers of clothes and consequently discover the necessity for the dances being conducted slowly.

Historical interpretation

This is the skill where children are taught about the different ways the past can be represented. Cooper (2002) states that this can be a neglected area of the curriculum but explores in some depth how stories can be used as a useful tool by which the beginnings of interpretations can be introduced. She discusses how different versions of stories can be utilized to show different representations of the same theme. She also talks about using different versions of stories in comics and alternative versions of stories about real people as other ways into the theme of interpreting the past. The Qualifications and Curriculum Authority (QCA, 2002) advocate the use of play as a vehicle to develop interpretation of events. The QCA (2002) describe how one class explored Cabot's voyage to Newfoundland in 1497 and how the role-played interpretations of this event composed by different groups of children clearly helped to consolidate their knowledge. They also stress the importance of the use of story by suggesting that children show their interpretations of the past through retelling the story in different forms, this might be by painting a picture of it or creating a puppet show, for example.

Historical enquiry

This is the skill which requires children to ask and answer questions about the past using a range of sources. This is a fascinating part of the curriculum to teach and can involve children in stimulating activities which can start to mirror the processes undertaken by 'real historians'. Children can ask questions about the past via pictures, photographs, portraits, artefacts and visit to historical sites.

Photographs provide a really good source for stimulating discussion in children. Starting with more familiar photographs can initially engage children and teach them the required observational skills necessary for this type of investigation. For example, it is a positive experience to ask children to look at two pictures of the same room taken a few years apart to spot what has changed. Children initially observe that there might be changes in digital technology (e.g. TVs might have got bigger in width but smaller in depth due to the availability of flat-screen display panels, video players might have morphed into DVD recorders, games consoles attached to TVs have transformed into wireless entities). While this might not be seen as 'history' in the traditional sense, activities like these do capture the interest of a class and require them to develop the skills of observation and investigation of change that are useful in exploring more complex historical pictures. As children become used to observing and analyzing pictures they can be introduced to the more distant past. Photographs from the nineteenth century are another accessible source of investigating the past. Asking children to look at photographs of this nature and to write a set of questions about the picture is a useful way of establishing initial analytical skills and encouraging children to ask investigative questions that begin with 'why', 'when' and 'where'.

Observation skills are key when using other types of artefacts. Taking children on walks and giving them sufficient time to make a careful drawing can be a useful exercise. Visiting sites of historical interest not just once but on several occasions, if possible, can give a view into the past. As Low-Beer and Blythe (1990: 34) state, the 'imperfection of sources of evidence for the past is well illustrated by a visit, for example, to a ruined monastery. On these occasions the detective skills of the historian are being developed'.

Organization and communication

This is about the way children express their thoughts in order to demonstrate their historical understanding. For young children the 'communication' aspect of this is a key skill, in that spoken word rather than literal representation of this might be important due to their inability to record information in the written form. The tangible product or 'work' that a young child produces might not be a good representation of the oral explanation that accompanies an investigation; the final piece of work will also be dependent on the maturity of the individual child's emerging literacy skills. Children of this age need to be given a variety of opportunities to show their understanding of a theme; this includes speaking and listening, jottings and artistic communication strategies as well as formal pieces of writing.

Conclusion

Historical understanding has an important place in the learning experience of young children. Giving children the opportunity to experience historical processes has benefits that can be realized right across the curriculum. Understanding a sense of time in their own lives and of those that came before allows children to develop empathy, cause and effect and sees the beginnings of cultural understanding. To deny the place of history in the curriculum at this stage would make the learning experience of children a poorer, less creative one. Far from being a dry subject, history can be something that stimulates the curiosity and imagination of children. As history does not become a discrete subject until Key Stage 1 and is approached in a cross-curricular manner in the foundation stage, practitioners should be fully secure in their understanding of the value of teaching emerging historical skills in order that they are sufficiently recognized during this stage of a child's learning experience.

References

Carle, E. (2002). *The very hungry caterpillar.* (Picture Puffins). London: Puffin Books

Cooper, H (2002) *History in the Early Years.* London: RoutledgeFalmer

Cooper, H (2007) *History 3–11: A Guide for Teachers.* Oxon: David Fulton Publishers Ltd

Cox, K. and Hughes, P. (1998) History and Children's Fiction in Hoodless, P. (ed) *History and English in the Primary Curriculum. Exploiting the Links.* London: Routledge

DCSF (2008) *Practice Guidance for the Early Years Foundation Stage: Setting the Standards for Learning, Development and Care for Children from Birth to Five.* London: Department for Children, Schools and Families

DCSF (2007) *Statutory Framework for the Early Years Foundation Stage.* London: Department for Children, Schools and Families

DFEE and QCA (1999) *The National Curriculum.* London: Crown Copyright and QCA

Hoodless (2008) *Teaching History in Primary School.* Exeter: Learning Matters

Low-Beer, A., Blyth, J. E. (1990) *Teaching history to younger children. Revised. (Teaching of History; no.52.).* London: Historical Association

O' Hara, L. and O'Hara, M. (2001) *Teaching History 3–11.* London: Continuum

Rose, J. (2009) *Independent Review of the Primary Curriculum: Final Report.* Available: http://publications.teachernet.gov.uk (accessed July 2009)

QCA, (2002) Innovating with History: How to teach about interpretations at Key Stages 1 to 3. Available from: http://www.qcda.gov.uk/history/innovating/improving_learning/interpretations/il-int8c.htm (accessed July 2009)

Waddell, M. and Benson, P. (1992). *Owl Babies.* London: Walker Books

Wood, L. and Holden, C. (1995) *Teaching Early Years History.* Cambridge: Chris Kington Publishing

5 Place

Introduction

Places are all around us; from the moment we are born we start to experience places. Children's turning, crawling, toddling and walking in their home environment introduces them to features, locations and movement.

(Catling, 2001: 1)

Inherently, places will have physical, human and environmental characteristics which together contribute to the uniqueness of a particular place or location.

Children's knowledge and understanding of places is affected by a number of factors. These can be broadly categorized into two main groups;

1 Direct experiences and
2 Indirect experiences

It is through these experiences that children come to develop a 'sense of place'. Children's learning about place in first hand situations will occur through the use of their senses. For newborn babies, amongst some of the things they may first *see* are a parent, a medical practitioner or the 'space' or 'environment' they are in. They may *feel* arms wrapped around them, the sensation from a warm blanket and/or *hear* the sounds in the room around them. All these feelings are connected to places.

When considering place understanding, it is important to develop children's cognitive sense of place as well as affective sense of place. Children's interactions with places are intimately bound up with their visits or those of relatives or friends. Places may be of interest because they know someone there, they are associated with the person who took them there, or they met a person who captured their imagination describing somewhere. These may be familiar, everyday places or far distant places but they are places that remain in children's minds because of their connections with people and events (Catling, 1988).

Developing knowledge and understanding of 'place' is a multifaceted area of learning. It involves thinking about children's:

- experiences of environments – past, present and future, including those in the educational setting;
- views and attitudes towards different places;
- interactions with places;
- learning experiences to best develop learning in this area.

Although in this chapter, some of these elements are considered as separate elements, in reality they are inextricably linked.

Development of place knowledge and understanding

The DCSF (2008, 87–88) state the following guidelines for the development of place knowledge and understanding in young children; From birth, children will start to explore the spaces around them through movement. By approximately 8 months, children are likely to take more interest in the outdoors and start to observe the actions of others and what different objects do. They then become more curious about their environment and by the age of 3 years, most children will enjoy playing with small world models. Between 30 and 50 months children are likely to show an interest in the world in which they live and ask questions about it, and the natural world, they may also notice differences between features of the local environment. In the latter stages of the Foundation Stage (40–60 months) children may find out about and identify features in the place they live and the natural world, find out about their environment, and talk about those features they like and dislike.

Of course, as we know, all children are different and to reflect this, the DCSF (2008) age ranges have been overlapped in the Early Years Foundation Stage to create broad developmental phases. This emphasizes that each child's progress is individual and that different children develop at different rates. Children do not suddenly move from one phase to another, and they do not make progress in all areas at the same time.

Case study

Paula – age 3 (displaying some understanding of place above her age phase).

The EYFS (DCSF, 2008, 87–88) recommends effective practice for developing place understanding for children between 30 and 50 months to include;

- Arousing awareness of features of the environment in the setting and immediate local area, for example, make visits to shops or a park.
- Introduce vocabulary to enable children to talk about their observations and to ask questions.
- Encourage parents to provide vocabulary in their home language to support language development and reinforce understanding.

Paula is just 3 years old and she has shown interest in visits to the local shops, park and library for the last 12 months (i.e. in the previous age phase), with a growing awareness of the features of her local area. The Early Years Practitioners in Paula's Nursery have noticed her interest in this aspect of learning and used this as a stimulus to set up their role play area as a shop. The children were asked to choose which shop they would like it to be and what sort of things should be included in it. Some children were able to respond with appropriate suggestions and others were able to talk about the daily events in the shop. Most of the children were able to become involved in some way to visiting and participating in the role play area, especially after some modelling had taken place, with Paula being the customer and the Early

Years Practitioner being the shop keeper. Within their new 'supermarket' Paula was able to ask questions such as;

- How much is this?
- Do you have any bananas?
- What time do you close?

It is therefore evident that there has been some understanding of place in the development phase prior to her chronological phase. Consider how this might be developed in the reflective activity below.

Reflection for early career professional

- What further forms of assessment would you want to undertake to assess Paula's developmental stage in this area of learning?
- Can you relate this situation to something similar in your own setting?
- How would you further develop Paula's and the child's learning experiences in your settings?

Reflection for leader/manager

- How can you effectively consider and implement the development of all children's learning within this area of learning in your setting?
- Can you lead your team in creating a thought shower of how place understanding could be developed within your setting? Include the likely steps you would like the children to take in the learning process and how this could be facilitated.

Knowledge, understanding, skills and attitudes

When talking about places, it is important to set the context of the place being studied. Where is it? How might it be connected to other places? How far away is it? How might we get there? How long would it take to get there? Where is it near? These are all questions we may consider asking before studying the area in more depth. Other aspects of place that might be studied are considered under the key questions later in this section.

Within the multifaceted aspect of 'place' learning, we need to consider how children's knowledge and understanding of place can be developed, but it is also vitally important to consider the attitudes children have. Jenner (2005) feels that children should be given the opportunity to learn about an overseas country, to have their ideas challenged, so that they are prepared to accept and nurture the multicultural society in which we live from a young age. Wood (2006) notes, that in today's world, children are exposed, from a very young age, to media influences, travel and attitudes and opinions of people around them. I would suggest that educational settings should therefore give explicit consideration to the global dimension.

Case study

An infant school had identified in their school development plan, that an aspect of learning which they wished to develop within their school was the global dimension. They had recognized that this was not a straightforward task so went about seeking advice on how this could be done appropriately. The school had allocated specific time and money in aiming to ensure the development was as successful as possible. First, they decided what particular aspects of learning they wished to focus on with the young children in their setting and how the outcomes could be produced successfully. The school decided to approach learning in a cross-curricular way and involved professionals with subject expertise, the local community with specific knowledge, experience and understanding of distant places and specialists in dance, music and food from the places being studied. For example, the children were taught some traditional dancing, tasted food from around the world (cooked by people with first hand experiences of place), Places were set in context with their location and varied aspects were considered, e.g. how might it feel to live in the town and how it might feel to live in the country. Children also related what they were learning to their home environment, and became aware that places are dynamic entities in which we may obtain a flavour of life but not the full picture. Related to this, children were encouraged to ask their own questions. The schools are now considering setting up the school in a distant place to make learning more 'real' for the children.

Practical tasks

Develop an activity to incorporate learning involving the global dimension in your setting.

Evaluate the activity and identify how successful it was in,

- developing children's understanding of place;
- developing positive attitudes and dealing with children's misconceptions about places,
- providing 'real' experiences for the children.

Wiegand (1992), notifies us that there are a great deal of methodological problems in attempting to identify just what children know and feel about entities (such as countries for example) which are conceptually fairly difficult to handle. He goes on to explain that children's understanding of places is the result of a complex relationship between development in the cognitive and affective domains. Reciprocity (the ability to look at things from someone else's point of view) is achieved once children are able to see that others make decisions based on how it appears to them, which is not necessarily the same as how things might seem to us. The child may begin with the idea that his/her ideas are the only ones possible (egocentricity). This does not mean that the child is selfish, but could be a developmental stage. For example the child may assume that someone else's knowledge of the local park is the same as theirs. According to this theory, the child would then later pass through a stage of sociocentricity (where the prevailing attitudes of those in the child's immediate surroundings are accepted or they are able to see the point of view of their immediate social group) to the reciprocity stage, where they can accept the views of others although they may be different to their own.

Piaget and Weil (1951) say that the main problem is not to identify what must or must not be taught, it is to discover how to develop that reciprocity in thought and action which is vital to the attainment of impartiality and affective understanding.

Robertson (2007) has suggested that the attitudes and skills needed to make a positive contribution to making the world a fairer and more sustainable place in the future need to be encouraged and developed from an early age because research shows (e.g. Milner, 1983 and Dixon, 1977) that many of the attitudes and skills learnt by children at the Foundation Stage are there to stay.

Ofsted (2008), states the following characteristics of schools where pupils' understanding of the global dimension is good.

- Links are made between fair trade and exploitation, poverty, wealth and interdependence.
- Good resources about another country are often used in lessons: for example, pupils' learning about another country is enhanced through a teacher's personal connections or pupils' own experiences or background heritage.
- Education for sustainable development is central to the school's philosophy, with pupils studying topics such as global warming, sustainability and the impact of their actions at local, national and global levels.
- The geography curriculum includes units of work on distant places.

Naturally, how the above fit in with an Early Years Curriculum would need careful consideration. I would suggest that themes such as the 3Rs (reduce, reuse, recycle), a growing garden (with the inclusion of edible products), aspects of citizenship and practitioners and pupils experiences of places could all be good starting points with young children.

One practitioner I saw prepared a starter activity for the children which motivated them to start recycling. The practitioner spoke to the caretaker of the school about leaving 'rubbish' (carefully selected of course) in their enclosed outside area for a lesson with the children. To make the learning more real for the children they invited the caretaker into the classroom to introduce the problem (real life context). The caretaker came into the room and said to the children,

> "I have got a little problem that I hope you can help me with? There has been quite a strong wind in the night and there seems to be rather a lot of rubbish all over the outside area (gasps from children). I would be very grateful if you could help me to tidy it up."

After which the children went and collected the rubbish (remember to consider health and safety) and put it into containers to bring back into the classroom. Once back in the classroom the teacher then discussed whether all the rubbish needed to go into the dustbin and it was then sorted according to the local recycling bins they have in their area.

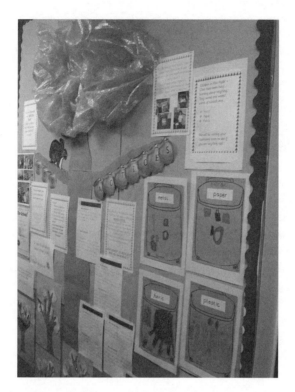

Photograph 5.1 Children learning about recycling (© Emma Jordan)

Blyth (1984: 45.) states;

"Young people are more influenced by how information is taught than what information is taught."

Within learning generally, and specifically place learning, this might include actions such as;

- Finding out children's current knowledge and misconceptions before starting a place based study. In this way, the teacher can consider ways to address

misconceptions and develop children's understanding, knowledge, skills and attitudes in a positive way
- Ensuring that appropriate resources are being used
- When exploring anything outside the pupils' direct experience, provide them with a context on which to pin the ideas so that they can make sense of what they are learning (Stanton, 2005)
- If possible using people's direct experience of place (places that people have visited)
- In this way, we would aim to develop children's knowledge, understanding, skills and attitudes in a positive way.

In line with this I would like to suggest some adaptations of the key questions for geography (Foley and Janikoun 1996:1) are given below, with adaptations in italics);

- Where is this place?
- What is this place like? *What might this place be like, How do we know?*
- Why is this place as it is? *What might have made this place like it is?*
- How is this place connected to other places? *What connections can we find to link this place to other places?*
- How is this place changing? *What can we find out about how this place is changing?*
- What is it like to be in this place? *What might it be like to be in this place?*
- How is this place similar to or different from another place? *How might this place be similar to or different to . . . ?*

By adapting the questions it is hoped that this will help towards children realizing that there is no definitive answer; we can find out a certain amount of information about places but without visiting the place itself there is always going to be more information to learn. We want them to have a desire to learn and find out more and ultimately realize that places are dynamic as they interact with people and the environment.

Other questions you may wish to be considered within a place study could include;

- What do we know about what this place used to be like?
- How can we represent this place in different forms? E.g. maps, pictures, 3D models.
- What do we like/dislike about this place? (Need to be sensitive here to children's experiences and feelings. For example if you are doing a local area study it is highly probably that many children will live in the area. If you decide it is appropriate to

talk about likes and dislikes you need to carefully consider what you are going to discuss and how it is going to be managed. For example you may decide to limit this to the school grounds).

- Would it be suitable to carry out an investigation/enquiry in this area?

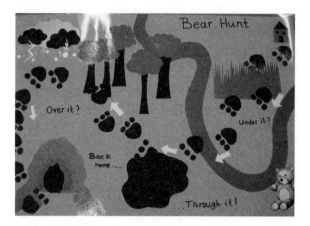

Photograph 5.2 Going on a bear hunt

Case study

An infant school based their first unit of work for Year 1 (transition unit) on the QCA (1998) Geography Scheme of Work: Around Our School, The Local Area. They do not follow the unit directly, realizing that the scheme was intended to be adapted to suit individual and school circumstances. As part of a transition unit between the Foundation Stage and Year 1, they consider the practical elements of the topic very important. They followed a key question approach and some of the questions that were included in their topic are outlined below;

- What do we already know about the local area and what would we like to find out? This includes children looking at the school and key features on a Google Earth Map. Children also look at a variety of photographs of their local area, to see which features they recognize and which they don't. They then go on a discovery walk to find the features they don't recognize.
- What is our favourite place in our local area. This forms part of a large classroom display, where each child draws or photographs a picture of their favourite place which is then added to the correct place on a large map.

Case study—Cont'd

- The children also look at changes in the local area, and realize that places undergo changes. In some years, this has led to enquiry-based work e.g. What effect will the new Tescos have on the local area (positive and negative)?

Reflection for early career professional

- From reading the above, are there any ways you would change or adapt the work you do on place studies (local and distant)?
- Can you think of some enquiry-based topics children could carry out either in the setting or local area (e.g. How can we improve our outside area?)

Reflection for leader/ manager

- What do you consider to be the advantages and disadvantages of a question-based approach, such as the one outlined above?
- How could you develop a scheme of work such as this in your setting to make it appropriate to your individual setting circumstances?
- Children's knowledge, understanding, skills and attitudes about their local area vary widely. What effective methods of differentiation/individual provision could you make?

The educational setting and place

It is important within an educational setting to have appropriate indoor and outdoor areas for the children to access and use. Practitioners taking part in a Teachers TV Programme (2008) emphasized the need for an enabling environment within the educational setting. They stated that the environment has a key role in supporting and extending children's development and learning. For example, children need to feel comfortable to explore places, find familiar places, revisit places and find their own secure place where they can perform, sit with a friend, paint or play for example.

Jarman (2007) warns that the conventional busy and stimulating environment of an educational setting isn't always the best place for the children, and that if it is too cluttered or over stimulating with excessive displays hanging from everywhere it can be too much for the children to absorb. She emphasizes the fact that she is *not* encouraging people to have dull classrooms. Therefore, what she suggests is that the way we offer the environment to children is critical in terms of their decision making, language development and confidence. She encourages practitioners to consider the following with regards to the role of their setting (Jarman, 2007: PowerPoint),

- the whole space inside and out
- screening off areas
- creating flexible spaces
- the need for private, cosy spaces
- the positioning of activities
- the child's perspective
- do you always want to be with other people or are there times when you'd rather be by yourself?
- how can we create space for individual thought, shared conversation and cooperation?

Practical task

Make a plan of how you would like to change the environment for your setting, taking into consideration the above advice. Also consider;

- Changes in your curriculum aims/goals for the setting at the time of the changes
- Resourcing
- The needs of your pupils and practitioners
- Draw out a plan of your suggested changes and display in a suitable place so comments and suggestions can be added. Implement the changes and evaluate how successful it was in terms of;
- Facilitating your aims and objectives for learning
- The development of the setting itself and place understanding/knowledge/attitudes
- Strengths and weaknesses of the changes that will need to be considered in the future. You may also wish to consider the suggestions outlined below in any future modifications.

Jarman (2007; PowerPoint) also suggests that the influence of unconnected noise such as a television or radio and the impact that this can have on the child's ability to listen and hold a conversation should be considered. She gives some of the following tips;

- Deep, 'warm' colours give learning spaces an intimate, cosy feeling.
- Light, 'cool' colours make a room seem more spacious and have a calming effect.
- It is a mistake to 'go overboard' with lots of bright, primary colours. This is just as bad as an all black and white room.
- Clean, clear, light colours are usually best for a learning atmosphere.
- Always have a low-light corner or darker area.
- Muted light can be relaxing, cosy and safe and enables children to settle into speaking and listening activities in a comfortable environment.
- Use drapes, blinds and nets to diffuse light or to add a change of hue to the light in your space.
- Natural light is a magical resource. Think about the light at different times of the day and the seasons. Don't let bulky curtains block the source of light.

When thinking about the educational setting in developing children's sense of place, it is vital of course, as mentioned briefly above, to consider the outdoor area. The Institute for Outdoor Learning (*http://www.outdoor-learning.org/*) states that learning outdoors is an engaging, effective and enjoyable form of learning, whether the emphasis is personal, social or environmental, or is about learning itself. Outdoor Learning provides first hand experience for learning about our natural world. It is also a powerful medium for personal, organizational and cultural change. Many socially useful purposes are readily achieved through Outdoor Learning.

There is evidence that pupils can benefit from experiences outside. For example, Ofsted (2004: 2) states that;

> "Outdoor education gives depth to the curriculum and makes an important contribution to students' physical, personal and social education. Factors contributing to good-quality teaching outdoors include small group size, teachers' specialist knowledge and their ability to adapt tasks to provide an appropriate challenge for students."

Over fairly recent years, there have been a number of awards and grants available to schools for developing the learning environment. These have included competitions run by local newspapers, councils and businesses for example. There are also a range of established schemes as outlined below;

Photograph 5.3 Children in the outdoor environment of their setting

Eco-Schools is an international award programme that guides schools on their sustainable journey, providing a framework to help embed these principles into the heart of school life. How this works from school to school will vary. For example, one school states some of the benefits of being an Eco-School as;

- Most of the children live in flats but can garden at school
- Involving children of all abilities
- Providing excellent opportunities for active learning
- A whole-school approach to planning and the sharing of skills between teachers
- Work linking to all 5 of the Every Child Matters outcomes and
- Work helping the school achieve Healthy Schools status (Southwark, 2009).

More information about Eco-Schools can be found on their website (Eco-Schools, 2009).

The **Forest Schools** philosophy is to encourage and inspire individuals through positive outdoor experiences. By participating in engaging, motivating and achievable tasks and activities in a woodland environment they believe each participant has an opportunity to develop intrinsic motivation, sound emotional and social skills. Children, say Forest Schools, need time to thoroughly explore their thoughts, feelings and relationships. This time and reflective practice develops understanding of the world, the environment, imagination and senses and everything within it through the use of emotions (see Forest Schools, 2009).

Learning through Landscapes helps schools and early years settings make the most of their outdoor spaces for play and learning (Learning through Landscapes, 2009). They can help with;

- Supporting delivery of all aspects of the curriculum in a stimulating, meaningful and fun way
- Creating genuine participation opportunities
- Increasing learning and play opportunities
- Improving the environment for children and staff alike, making a better, happier place to be and developing a positive, caring ethos
- Providing a wide range of formal and informal opportunities for physical activity, improving health, well-being and motivation to learn.
- Identifying how to make physical changes to your grounds, and find people who can help you.

Also, the **Geographical Association's Primary Quality Mark** states that one of the reasons to apply is to celebrate the characteristics of geography in your school, i.e. what the learning environment looks like and what a rich, exciting experience your geography is giving children (North and Richardson, 2008). See the Primary Quality Mark pages on the Geographical Association's website (GA, 2009).

Case study

Le Cateau Community Primary School has achieved a leading aspect award (June 2006) and is committed to enhancing outdoor provision for Early Years pupils. It has expanded and developed the quality and range of outdoor learning opportunities. The children wear appropriate outdoor all-weather clothing bought by the school, so no pupil is disadvantaged. The high quality of provision has been recognized by OFSTED and the Local Education Authority (LEA), who recommend other schools interested in developing their own Early Years outdoor areas to visit Le Cateau and see good practice.

Provision includes the following key areas of learning:

- digging and planting in designated garden areas
- harvesting their own fruit
- imaginative role play in the outdoor house
- imaginative role play in the outdoor shop/garage
- exploring the mini maze and pathways around the outdoor play area
- using the "Sound Area" with its range of objects and musical instruments
- exploring the tunnels created by the camouflage netting
- using the bicycles and scooters on a well-laid out road system complete with road signs
- developing ball skills (e.g. throwing and catching)
- developing physical skills through using the climbing equipment and swing
- observing minibeasts and habitats
- mark making
- developing numeracy skills (e.g. in the outdoor shop, etc).

Since winning the award, the school has also developed the outdoor area even further with a huge 'beach area', a big digging area and a construction area using 'bread' crates and planks (see Leading Aspect Award, 2009).

It is important to remember that just because the outdoor environment is being used it doesn't necessarily mean that learning is going to be effective, beneficial or suited to everyone. One of the most important considerations is, of course, the needs of the children. As we know, the needs of children vary widely and so do the places that they are most likely to thrive and develop. For example, the Institute of Outdoor Learning suggests that learners who usually struggle can excel in the outdoor classroom which provides such a different climate for learning that learners often become motivated and capable learners in the outdoors. Teachers are frequently surprised by the abilities and interest shown by 'poorly performing' students when in the outdoors, and by the extent to which Outdoor Learning has awakened their potential. We should provide variety of environments and consider how often these should be changed, evaluate the success and impact of the environments created and crucially involve the children in the decision making about their learning environment.

Reflective tasks

Reflection for early career professional

- Observe and note how the children in your setting react to different environments/places. You may wish to choose an environment outlined by the suggestions in this chapter. How do you think the children's experiences influenced these results?

Reflection for leader/ manager

Consider your educational setting and how the children in your setting may react differently to known and unknown environments. Emotions are likely to be attached to places. It is therefore important to consider how children's different emotional experiences may affect their behaviour in different settings.

- What considerations will this lead you to when organizing and arranging the environment in your setting?

Resources

There are a wide variety of resources that can be used in relation to place learning. These resources will have implications on learning and teaching about places. The resources that you choose will of course be dependent on the children in your setting and the learning outcomes you wish to achieve. Perhaps the predominant resource or the one likely to be used a great deal in your setting is the local environment. Other resources that you may wish to consider for place studies include:

- Recording equipment, such as data loggers, digital cameras/video, and dicta-phones (for a sound walk for example)
- Teacher drawn maps of the classroom, school, local area or fictional place,
- Large scale maps that show features that may be recognized by young children
- Barnaby Bear (or similar) to take on visits
- Photographs and pictures of the local area
- Perspex box for introducing children to the concept of an aerial view
- Google Earth or Windows Live Local
- Webcams

- Clothing suitable for outdoors
- Storybooks
- Road safety role play equipment
- Materials to make 3D models of aspects of your local area
- Information books
- Fieldwork
- For slightly older children handheld technologies such as Personal Digital Assistants (PDAs) are becoming more widely used in schools. Gayler, S. (1997, unpublished) from WildKnowledge says children grow up surrounded by technology; their acceptance of it as a way to engage, play games, communicate, learn, research and walk away from is fairly advanced. Children as young as 2 or 3 can easily grasp the concepts of simple games on handheld gaming devices such as the Nintendo DS; what they are learning from an early age is how to use a stylus and make marks on a screen, and cause and effect processes, not dissimilar to holding a pencil or crayon and making marks on paper, the same end result, just a different medium. When it comes to a more specific task of learning, the technology should be considered as just another tool to aid the learning, and not as a replacement for other traditional methods. The important thing to consider is that many of the children entering school at the age of 4 or 5 are already equipped with technological skills, which are then not utilized in schools. For mainstream learning where there is device ownership in the school, then in reality you wouldn't be deploying mobile devices much before Year 5. Although of course, there is a great deal of technological learning outlined above that can take place before this.

When studying 'distant' places it is almost certain that secondary sources of information will need to be used. This brings with it all sorts of issues. There are a number of questions you may want to ask yourself when considering which resources to use. Some of these questions may also be applicable to local area studies, with the key difference with distant places being the lack of direct experiences that pupils will have. Questions to ask include;

- How old are the resources?
- Have they been altered in any way?
- Do they enable the children to achieve what was desired?
- Do they re-inforce stereotypical images?
- Are they an accurate representation of the place?
- Has the place changed and how do we know?

It may be difficult to find new, up-to-date, unaltered, non-stereotypical resources that can depict a place accurately but I believe it is still important to consider these things. In this way, we can make children aware that what we may be learning about a place is likely not to give us the 'full picture'. We can talk about resources we use with the children and relate this to journeys they may have been on.

In my experience, a role play area within an Early Years setting will not be particularly successful unless there is some kind of modelling taking place or previous experience related to how the area might be used. It is then from these models that children will not only start to imitate what they have seen, but bring in things from their experiences and imagination. Dean and Jackson (2003) believe that supporting interaction in children's spontaneous play is complex and requires practitioners not only to provide high quality resources, but to listen and play alongside the children, to observe, understand and respond to children appropriately. When interaction is effective it supports learning by helping the child to express, explore, investigate and share their ideas, discuss and develop vocabulary, raise and ask questions, extend and try out new ideas, persist in their learning, exploring problems and finding solutions.

Ofsted (2008) gives an example of how a school encourages positive experiences in the Reception class, where the teachers use stories, outdoor activities and role play to develop children's knowledge and understanding of the world. In Key Stage 1 (DfES, 1999), pupils continue to develop the skills of observation and enquiry through the many opportunities to learn outside the classroom. By the end of the key stage, pupils know the countries of the UK, the location of their home town, sea/land and hot/cold regions and can identify them on world maps. They use photographs showing different environments and seasons and can describe differences between their location and contrasting locations. It is important that skills such as these develop progressively.

Maps are an important source of information for learning about places. But as you know we cannot expect very young children to start reading and interpreting complicated maps. What I believe is important is a steady progression in map skills throughout a child's education. Blades et al (2007) states that what has intrigued some geographers and psychologists is whether very young children have any knowledge of maps, even before any formal teaching has taken place. Some experts on child development, like Jean Piaget (in Blades et al., 2007), believed that children would have little or no ability to understand a map until after the age of seven or eight years. More recently, people such as Jim Blaut have taken a different view. According to Blaut (in Blades et al., 2007), very young children should be able to look at an image, like an aerial photograph of a town, and see it for what it represents. Several years ago Blaut demonstrated the abilities of young children by asking them to describe what they could see in black and white aerial photographs of urban landscapes. He found that children down to about five years of age could spontaneously name what they saw as roads, houses, buildings, trees, parks and other geographic features. Such an immediate understanding suggested that children do not have any difficulty interpreting an aerial perspective, and many geographers have concluded that children's very good ability to interpret representations like aerial photographs could be the basis for understanding simple maps. Another element of research by Blades et al. (2007) demonstrated that even nursery-school-age children could recognize and understand aerial photographs – an age group much younger than previously tested. This finding supported Blaut's idea that very young children, without any specific training, can look at a photograph taken from above and spontaneously interpret it as a representation of the world. Although children are not explicitly shown aerial views by their parents or teachers, even very young children may see numerous landscape views in the course of reading picture books and watching television, films, and cartoons. These media are full of stories and illustrations of flying carpets, flying superheroes, and even flying snowmen. Children also see many factual programmes – for instance, about animals, birds or the environment – that may include numerous aerial views. These programmes often juxtapose a ground-level scene with, a second later, a view from an aerial perspective.

There are of course many maps available now on the Internet, as well as photographs and videos which need consideration as outlined in the resources section of this chapter. The ICT in the Early Years website informs us that children are immersed in technologically-rich environments, both in their homes, nurseries/schools and in the local environment; there are remote controls for television and video sets, toys that have buttons and buzzers, phones and mobile phones, washing machines, microwaves and other machines that require programming, computers, photocopiers, answer phones, security keypads for entry, automatic doors, ticket machines, cash machines, bar-code scanners, digital tills and weighing machines, security cameras, the list can go on and on. In exploring the local area, you could try taking an ICT walk with children identifying ICT and related uses in their environments such as street lights, signals, automatic doors, ticket machines. It can be quite an eye-opener and can lead to setting up role-play areas. Technology can also support knowledge and understanding of the world.

Practical tasks

Carry out an audit of the resources that you have in your setting that could be used in teaching and learning about places (see Schools Resource. Audit-Commission, 2009). A Managing School resources self-evaluation tool which you may wish to use in this process). With your colleagues, prioritize any items you wish to buy from your budget, taking into consideration;

- Topics/themes you may be covering
- Experiences of the practitioners/pupils
- Pupil input/ideas
- Sources of alternative funding/materials that may be available

---

Play

Through play younger children will act out the actions and places they see and encounter, through replicating and enhancing the rituals of journeys, imagining one space as another, perhaps a shop or school. They re-create spaces into miniature environments in which to enact fantasies. Imitative play draws on the reality children see around them. Fantasy play is built from some of this reality but also from stories told and read to them and from television for example. Through imaginative activities children are also engaged in making sense of the world about them (Catling, 2001).

Dean and Jackson (2003), state that early play experiences provide the foundations for later learning. Through play, in a secure environment with effective adult support, children can explore, develop and represent learning experiences that help them make sense of the world.

Conclusion

It is clear then, that there are many considerations to the development of place learning – encompassing knowledge, understanding, skills and attitudes. Finding out children's current perceptions in these areas are crucial if successful progress is to be made. We need to consider the sort of questions we ask and the resources we use. Linked to this, we need to check the accuracy and reliability of resources and the 'outside influences' that may alter children's perceptions of place. It is also helpful to think about children's direct and indirect experiences of place, and how we might provide these in our educational setting. We want to make appropriate links to the real world and be able to express how exciting it is to find out about places, that they are dynamic entities – we can find out some things about places in the past and the present and want to find out more about them in the future and ultimately lead towards life-long learning.

References

Blades, M., Spencer, C. and Plester, B. (2007) Helping very young children to start learning about maps, *Mapping News 32* Summer 2007. Southampton: Ordnance Survey

Blyth, J. (1984) *Place and Time with Children 5 to 9.* London: Routledge Kegan & Paul

Catling, S. (1988) Children and Geography in *Geographical Work in Primary and Middle Schools,* (ed) David Mills, 9–18. Sheffield: The Geographical Association

Catling, S. (2001) Primary Geography Matters keynote paper to the *IGU Commission on Geographical Education Regional Symposium, Innovative Practices in Geographical Education,* Finland: Helsinki (also available *at* www.geography.org.uk/download/EVcatlingpgmat.doc)

Consalarium Blog – Scottish Centre for Games and Learning

DfES (2008) *The Early Years Foundation Stage; Setting the Standard for Learning, Development and Care for Children from Birth to Five; Practice Guidance.* London: DfES

Dean, K. and Jackson, E. (2003) A sense of place in *Primary Geographer Magazine,* April 2003. Sheffield: Geographical Association

Dixon, B. (1977) *Catching Them Young,* Pluto Press: London

Author (2008) EYFS Today – *Enabling Environments* Published: 19 May 2008, teachers tv: http://www.teachers.tv/video/27107

Eco-Schools (2009) Eco-Schools. http://www.eco-schools.org.uk/about/

Foley, M and Janikoun, J. (1996) *The Really Practical Guide to Primary Geography,* 2nd *Edition.* Cheltenham: Nelson Thornes

Forest Schools, (2009) Forest Schools. http://www.forestschools.com/

GA (Geographical Association), (2009) http://www.geography.org.uk/eyprimary/primaryqualitymark/

Homerton Nursery and Early Excellence Centre (2009) *ICT in the Early Years.* England: Cambridge http://foundation.e2bn.org/index.php?option=com_content&task=view&id=23&Itemid=27

Institute for Outdoor Learning (2009) What is Outdoor Learning? Why does Outdoor Learning Matter? Institute for Outdoor Learning: Carlisle. http://www.outdoor-learning.org/what_is_outdoor_learning/why_ol_matters.htm

Jarman, E. (2007) Communication Friendly Spaces – *NCMA Network Co-ordinator Support Seminar,* 10th May 2007

Jenner, F. (2005) Young Children's Perceptions of Distant Places in Research Reports from *The Geographical Association* http://www.geography.org.uk/resources/research/reports/

Lea, K. (2005) It's Good to get Global! Global Citizenship in the Early Years http://www.foundation-stage.info/newfsf/articles/visitors/FSFArticle_138.php

Leading Aspect Awards Website (2009): Case Studies

Le Cateau Community Primary School, North Yorkshire: June 2006 (achieved) http://www.leadingaspectaward.org.uk/casestudy/Le+Cateau+Community+Primary+School,+North+Yorkshire/488

Learning through Landscapes, (2009) http://www.ltl.org.uk/

Milner, (1983) http://www.foundation-stage.info/newfsf/articles/visitors/FSFArticle_138.php

North, W. and Richardson, P. Primary Geography Quality Mark, *The Geographical Association Magazine,* Autumn 2008 (10)

Ofsted (2004) Outdoor Education – Aspects of Good Practice Document Reference Number: HMI 2151 www.ofsted.gov.uk

Ofsted (2008) Geography In Schools: Changing Practice http://www.ofsted.gov.uk/Ofsted-home/News/Press-and-media/2008/January/Geography-in-schools-changing-practice/(language)/eng-GB

Piaget, J. & Weil, A. (1951). The Development in Children of the Idea of the Homeland and its Relation with other Countries, *International Social Science Bulletin,* 3, 561–578

Qualifications and Curriculum Authority (1998). *Geography at Key Stages 1 and 2.* QCA/DCSF: London

Robertson, (2007) http://www.foundation-stage.info/newfsf/articles/visitors/FSFArticle_138.php

Southwark, (2009) http://www.southwark.gov.uk/YourServices/educationandlearning/Environmental Education/ecoschools/charlesdickensecoschool.html

Stanton, L. (2005) Enquiry in the Early Years, *Primary Geographer* Spring edition. Sheffield: Geographical Association Teachers TV Journey Sticks, KS1/2 Geography, Published: 28 November 2007

Schools Resource Audit-Commission (2009) http://www.schoolsresource.audit-commission.gov.uk/system/default.htm

Underwood, L. (2005) Ranking Places in *Primary Geographer.* Sheffield: Geographical Association

Wiegand, P. (1992) *Places in the Primary School: Knowledge and Understanding of Places at Key Stages 1 and 2.* London: The Falmer Press

White, J. in http://www.teachingexpertise.com/articles/meeting-the-challenges-of-outdoor-provision-in-the-early-years-foundation-stage-2967

Wood, S. (2006) Learning About Distant Places at KS1, *Tidetalk Journal* www.tidec.org/Tidetalk/articles/distant%20places.html

Communities 6

Introduction

Young children belong to communities at a range of levels. They may have one, two or more parents or carers, siblings, and live with or near to members of a wider family including those from different generations. They can be a part of a greater community of friends and neighbours and can be members of playgroups and nurseries, clubs and religious organizations, or may be part of a small group of children looked after by a child-minder. These groupings all involve social networks.

Children are also members of physical communities in which they access services including shops, health centres and playgrounds. On a wider level, other communities are accessed through the broadcast media and these may include a broader range of cultural groups than a child physically encounters on a day-to-day basis. Through community-based relationships children learn some of the features of being human (through showing and experiencing care and friendship) and begin to understand that their behaviour and attitudes can have consequences.

Communities bring the opportunity to learn about the wants and needs of others and to understand that people can share similarities or exhibit differences. We each begin to form our identity through our experience of community: learning what we like and dislike, how to cooperate and share, what it means to be respectful and to show care, and how to cope with differences and disagreement. This chapter explores these areas, relating them to the early learning goals and providing examples of children's experiences. It considers how children begin to encounter and understand others, and how this relates to stages in theories of child development. It considers how young children move from dependency within their communities to begin to contribute to the societies of which they are members.

The importance of communities

A sense of community is essential to understanding what it means to be human. People do not normally live in isolation but in relation to others and in relationships with them. If we consider our own lives, we will identify ourselves through a range of roles and interactions with others. Asking the question 'Who am I?' may lead to a variety of answers including carer, professional, writer, artist, cook, neighbour, gardener or swimmer. We may be members of different organizations, we are involved in our workplace and will have different relationships based around family and friends groupings. Whether we are shy or outgoing, a great deal of our identity comes from being a part of different communities, both small and large.

Children are also members of different communities and as they grow become involved in an increasingly wide circle of experience and relationships. From birth this circle may be relatively small, focusing on primary carer(s). There may be secondary carers (for example grandparents, aunts or uncles), siblings, and family friends and neighbours. In time this circle grows to include a childcare setting, other community groups and personal friendships.

Community from birth to 3 years of age

Even from before their first words, children discover a great deal about language by listening to people talking. In their first year they develop secure attachments to special people such as carers, parents and family members. Their learning and interest in their environment is supported by a wide variety of experiences including all the senses. At this time it is important not only to speak with children but also to ask questions and to develop interaction with them. Children are receptive to different tones of voice, humour and laughter and the inflections involved in asking questions. Primary carers need to engage them in conversation, give explanations and show them new and exciting things. The tones associated with praise and affirmation are particularly important in developing a warm and caring relationship.

From 8–20 months children become mobile and discover new opportunities for exploration. It is at this time that they begin to relate to other people and to develop their social skills with those with whom they have a positive attachment (for a discussion of the idea of attachment see Chapter 1 of *Personal, Social and Emotional Development* in this series). They have a developing sense of self and are more able to express their feelings and needs. Interaction with others is key to supporting the development of their communication skills and the growth of their vocabulary.

From 16 months playing with other children is important. This helps them to learn how to cooperate with others and to understand other people's thoughts and feelings. Pretend play can help children learn about a range of possibilities and to try out new thoughts and ideas. From 22 months until the age of three years children develop self-confidence and a degree of independence, if appropriate adult support is given. This may be evidenced particularly in the areas of eating, toileting and dressing. Joining in conversations with children is important as they start to put together sentences. Play with other children develops with physical skills that usually include running, jumping and climbing: thus learning about safety and danger is important. During this period children are starting to learn how to interact with others and with their environment: both key elements of learning a sense of community

(Papalia, Gross and Feldman, 2003). A sense of the physical environment, learning what they like and dislike about that setting and finding out about the area in which they live, helps to develop a sense of place and of being part of a location. Being located in a particular place can bring a sense of belonging and security. Relating to others, and beginning to develop interactions with them, helps to develop further this sense of belonging and being accepted.

Case study

Kath, Mike and Helen were born within six weeks of each other. Their mothers attended the same antenatal class and maintained contact after the children were born. They meet weekly for coffee in each other's homes. Now aged 2 years, the children are developing at different rates. Kath plays with her own toys, showing no interest in the toys brought by the other children or in joining in with the others. Mike and Helen try out the different toys available but Helen frequently wants the toy that Mike is using currently and becomes easily distressed if he does not give way to her.

Reflection for early career professional

- What difficulties might children of this age face when being placed in this social setting? How might you address these issues?
- Is it appropriate to encourage all the children to interact with one another and how might you encourage this?
- How could you develop the situation outlined in the case study to help the children to play together and to relate?

Reflection for leader/manager

- What support and advice might you give to each parent/carer to help them to manage this situation?
- What concerns might Kath's parent have about her social development?
- How would you support professionals in your setting to build increasing levels of social interaction between children over time?

Community from 3 to 5 years of age

At this age the social skills of sharing and cooperating are developed through play with others including construction, games and make-believe. Children also learn about helping adults with everyday activities. From 3 – 4 years children are gaining in increased sense of their place in the community. With the ability to use longer and increasingly complex sentences comes the opportunity to converse more and to gain reassurance, support and guidance from adults. Helping to lay the table before a meal, planting seeds together or contributing to choices when shopping, all provide social opportunities to become involved in family life and to contribute to that small community.

From 40 months until the age of five years children build a greater sense of their own identity and their place in the wider world. They have a greater awareness of social customs and rules and can show tolerance and understanding towards others. Social skills are developed by playing in small groups and through shared activities with adults or peers. Sharing space and resources in the nursery provides social experiences that can promote the development of skills including patience, respect and turn taking. Small world activities provide the opportunity for imaginative play that includes the need to relate to others (Papalia, Gross and Feldman, 2003). In one school I saw a small world area set up as a farm yard in which children decided together which animals they wanted to keep, where the animals should be housed and who should be responsible for feeding them. Similarly, sharing in group activities such as singing action songs and reciting rhymes provides a shared experience which fosters a sense of belonging and mutual enjoyment. At this age children are developing an awareness of some of the differences between people in their community. Edwards and Lewis (1979) found that children aged 42 months could sort head-and-shoulders photographs of people into four categories successfully: little children, big children, parents and grandparents. This shows an awareness of the different generations that make up a community.

Case study

In one school in Lincolnshire children in the Early Years Foundation Stage developed individual books entitled *All About Me*. They found out how tall they were when they were born and compared this with their current height, using lengths of string to provide a visual representation. They found out where they were born and where their families came from. They also drew their family members and their favourite things. This enabled them to record aspects of their past and present lives and to identify some changes that had taken place over time. It also helped them to understand that different members of the class had come from different places and to see some of the differences and similarities in their lives.

Reflection for early career professional

- How could you encourage children to share and to record their interests and memories? Could you develop activities from this to value differences and to celebrate similarity?
- How would you develop a sense of community with the children and a shared sense of belonging?

Reflection for leader/manager

- How would you address any instances of intolerance or misunderstanding arising from differences amongst children or their family backgrounds?
- How would you support colleagues in valuing difference and diversity?
- What approach would you take if you found that a professional held views that were not in line with the equal opportunities policy of the setting?

This case study provides opportunities to address the requirement of the *Early Years Foundation Stage* that children should find out about past and present events in their own lives, and in those of their families and other people they know (DCSF, 2008). Importantly it provides the opportunity for children to start with their own experience and work outwards to that of others; beginning with the familiar and developing learning about less well-known information.

At the end of this stage children should be attaining the Early Learning Goals that I identify as relating to developing a sense of community (DCSF, 2008: 14, 15) and be able to:

- find out about, and identify, some features of living things, objects and events they observe (which, I suggest, includes an awareness of care, friendship, kindness and respect);
- ask questions about why things happen and how things work (which includes an awareness of the consequences of one's actions and those of others, and their impact on other people);
- find out about past and present events in their own lives, and in those of their families and other people they know;
- observe, find out about and identify features in the place they live and the natural world;
- find out about the environment, and talk about those features they like and dislike;
- begin to know about their own cultures and beliefs and those of other people.

These skills provide the basis for a developing understanding of community and help to create the opportunity to contribute to communities in increasing ways.

Transition to Key Stage 1 (5 to 7 years of age)

The transition from the Early Years Foundation Stage to Key Stage 1 is, at its best, a process rather than an event (Sanders et al, 2005). Schools should seek to develop similar routines, expectations and activities in Reception and Year 1. Children face transitions at different points in their development, including as they progress within settings or change setting. This process involves meeting new children and adults, becoming accustomed to new routines and gaining familiarity with new surroundings. Each of these is a part of becoming a member of a new or different community. Fabian and Dunlop (2002) suggest that such transition experiences affect children's abilities to adapt and learn. Particularly in a child's early years it is important for parents, carers and professionals to plan carefully for transitions in order to make them as smooth and trauma-free as possible, observing carefully their impact upon the child. As a part of this, it is key to consider how relationships are developing at a range of levels in order to ensure that a child is making good progress and adapting well to change (Pianta et al., 1999). These include:

- child to child;
- child to parent/carer;
- child to professional.

It is important to monitor concerns in any of these areas in order to maximize learning, development and a sense of security. Such security may be enhanced if the child has siblings or existing friendships in the new setting (Graham and Hill, 2003; Stephen and Cope, 2001; Margetts, 2003; Johnstone, 2002) or if they are already developing effective social skills. In a study of children moving from Reception to Year 1, Ofsted (2004) found that children generally viewed transition in a positive light but had some concerns, including some about workload. There is a danger that the move into Key Stage 1 diminishes the use of play, dialogue and open-ended questioning to support children's learning (Moyles et al., 2002; Siraj-Blatchford et al., 2002) and brings more formality, increased time sitting and listening and a more rigid structure provided by literary and numeracy lessons. It is important to consider how to develop the transition to this different pedagogical approach and how effective practice from Reception, which includes opportunities for children to initiate their own learning, can be built upon in the new setting.

At this stage children are making increasing contributions to the development of a sense of community. Their individual interests, likes and dislikes all add to the variety of the experience of playing, working, socializing and learning together. In addition, they are able to share their experience of their home communities and to appreciate the different experience of others. As children grow up they become more aware that people differ by ethnic origin. By the age of 4 or 5 years they may be able to identify basic differences, for example, between people who identify as black or white. However, an awareness of the constancy of ethnicity does not come until the ages of 8 or 9 years (about a year later than a sense of gender constancy). Aboud (1988) found that half the 6-year-olds shown photographs of an Italian-Canadian boy putting on native-American clothes thought that the pictures were of different boys. There can be a misunderstanding about how appearance affects who we are.

Finkelstein and Haskins (1983) found that 5-year-old kindergarten children in the USA showed marked preferences for playmates from their own ethnic group. However, when interacting with a peer the children did not behave differently when working with a child from the same or a different ethnic group. It is important to note that preference is not the same as prejudice: one may choose to play with children from the same ethnic group or of the same gender as oneself but also believe that all children are just as good as oneself and one's friends (Smith, Cowie and Blades, 2003). Prejudice requires a negative evaluation of others. Bringing children together in common activities provides one means to reduce any ethnic preference or prejudice in the classroom (Cowie et al., 1994).

Case study

In December, Joseph brought an eight-branched candelabra to school to show his class. His teacher asked him to explain why it was important and invited his mother to visit one afternoon to explain when the candles would be lit and why it was special to do this. The class learned about the Jewish festival of Hanukah and talked about the different times when they lit candles as a part of a celebration. Samuel explained that his family also lit candles every Friday evening at the start of the Jewish Sabbath; Amie had been given an Advent candle to burn each day in the time before Christmas; and Samir had recently blown out six candles on his birthday cake. Linda explained that her mum and dad sometimes lit candles if they had a special meal on Saturday evening, and that she and her brother were allowed to help to get the meal ready but went to bed early so that mum and dad could have some time to relax together. The children decided that they would light a candle at the start of each afternoon to have a special time together when one of them could choose a favourite song or rhyme.

Reflection for early career professional

- Review resources in your setting to establish how different cultures are presented.
- What questions or interventions do you think would help children to share aspects of the communities of which they are a part?
- How could you encourage children to feel confident and secure when coming across new ideas and experiences from communities or cultures different to their own?

Reflection for leader/manager

- Review the activities you provide for children in your setting. How do they encourage children to share different celebrations from their varied backgrounds and cultures?
- What opportunities do you provide to share celebrations from cultures different to those of the children?
- Evaluate ways in which you can communicate the importance of sharing stories and experiences from varied cultures with carers and parents.

Developing a sense of community

A sense of community can be developed by appreciating friendships and by considering how we help one another and cooperate. Children's experience of the learning environment brings an awareness that their behaviour and attitudes can have consequences. They become aware of the wants and needs of one another and they begin to develop a sense of self-identity that is shaped by the ways in which others respond to them. They are continually learning what they like and dislike, how to cooperate and share, what it means to be respectful and to show care, and how to cope with difference and disagreement.

Differences in any setting will be varied. Children will have different patterns of family life including having one or two parents, an extended family, a parent who lives away from them (due to divorce, the requirements of work, military service or imprisonment), some may have same sex parents, adoptive or foster parents, or be looked after by a different family member. Children will also live in diverse locations, in houses or flats, in trailers or on boats. They will come from a range of socio-economic backgrounds, have parents/carers or different ages, some will live in families where a member has a disability and others will be from different nationalities or ethnic backgrounds (Charlesworth, 2000; Morris and Woolley, 2008). At times we will be aware of some of these differences, but not always. It is therefore important to seek to make learning settings inclusive to reflect the diversity of the children in our care (both known and unknown diversity) and to reflect the diversity of the wider community and society in general. At first, this may appear to be a gargantuan task, but with thought and care it is possible to develop our approaches to inclusion and diversity in increasing measure. It is also important to remember that professionals come from a range of backgrounds and different communities and they also need to feel safe, appreciated and valued. This is important so that we help children to achieve the outcomes of the *Every Child Matters* agenda (DfES, 2004): to be healthy (which includes their mental health and well-being); enjoying and achieving; to stay safe, and to feel safe and secure in their learning environment; and being able to make a positive contribution, which itself requires them to feel valued by themselves and those around them.

One example illustrates the point (Woolley, 2008: 115,116):

I heard the story recently of a child that had been taught by their mum how to draw a house whenever the topic of 'homes' came up at school. The child learned to draw a square house with a pitched roof, four windows and a door (Tierney 2007, speaking at a conference to launch the North Lincolnshire Inclusion Strategy). The parent felt that there would be a stigma attached to the fact that they lived in a trailer as a part of a traveller community.

The idea that parents and carers are unwilling to identify as travellers because they feel that schools will make inappropriate judgements about them and their children shows how important it is for us, as professionals, to value the backgrounds of all our learners. Without this, children are not going to feel valued as a part of the community of our setting and are going to fail to thrive in the wider community. Mistrust, stereotypes and prejudice are all concepts which we must seek to address and to minimize.

Practical tasks

Using a story that illustrates a culture different to that of the children, for example *Samira's Eid* (Aktar, 2002), *The Friday Night's of Nana* (Hest, 2001) or *Lights for Gita* (Gilmore, 1994), share the experience of a child or family enjoying a time of celebration. Ask the children how the celebration is similar to and different from those that they share in their own families.

- How did the children relate to the different culture/community in the story?
- What did the children's responses and questions reveal about their under-standing of the difference and the ways in which they view other people?
- How can you build upon this experience to extend the children's knowledge and understanding of the world?
- How are various cultures, communities and countries represented in your setting through toys and games, picture books and displays?

The importance of community cohesion

The *Education and Inspections Act 2006* introduced a duty on all maintained schools in England to promote community cohesion and on Ofsted to report on the contributions made in this area. This duty on schools came into effect in September 2007 and the duty on Ofsted commenced in September 2008.

In July 2007 the government issued *Guidance on the Duty to Promote Community Cohesion*. This guidance states that all children can benefit from meaningful interaction and requires providers to consider how children can be given the opportunity to mix with and learn from those from different backgrounds. It suggests that making links with community organizations and with other schools can make this possible (DCSF, 2007).

The *Commission on Integration and Cohesion* (2007: 112) identified different elements associated with the term community. The focus on meeting with members of the community is particularly key to this process, as:

> Meaningful contact between people from different groups has been shown to break down stereotypes and prejudice. Contact is meaningful when: conversations go beyond surface friendliness; in which people exchange personal information or talk about each other's differences and identities; people share a common goal or share an interest; and they are sustained long-term (so one off or chance meetings are unlikely to make much difference). Importantly, this theory suggests that keeping difference in the forefront of people's minds when they are interacting across groups helps them to generalize what they have experienced – so they will take from their encounter not just a revised view of an individual, but of a whole group.

Such interactions can work on a range of levels, including:

- Within a setting/school (by meeting with children of different ages to share in activities);
- Setting to setting (through collaboration between staff and by bringing together children to share in activities);
- Setting to parents/carers and the wider community (through the use of visitors to the setting or visits undertaken by the children);
- Setting to community services (through meeting with representatives e.g. local councillors, religious leaders, the police, fire service, local shops or care homes).

These different levels provide opportunities for children to meet a range of people and to learn about their lives and work. This may be at the level of cooperating with, or being supported by, an older child as part of an activity, or learning about road safety or stranger danger from a visiting police officer. It might also involve visiting the local store or supermarket to learn about shopping, money or where our food comes from. This also links to the need for children to observe, find out about and identify features in the place they

Photograph 6.1 Developing community cohesion in the early years (© P. Hopkins)

live (DCSF, 2008). Each opportunity provides the chance to learn about those living or working in the local area, to get to know key people and to understand that others contribute a great deal to our day-to-day lives. This is all a part of developing a sense of community and of knowing and understanding more about the world and how it functions (Woolley and Hanson, 2008). This relates to the requirement that children should begin to know about their own cultures and beliefs and those of other people (DCSF, 2008). This concept is explored in more detail in Chapter 6 of *Personal, Social and Emotional Development* in this series of books.

Learning about people in the local community can help to minimize the development of stereotypes by which children label people according to the groups to which they seem to belong rather than seeing them as individuals. For example, it is important that children see older people as persons in their own right rather than presuming that they have certain characteristics or abilities because of their age. Linden (1998) suggests that stereotypes are usually unfavourable, depend on a belief that others' groups are less varied than one's own and are often maintained despite personal experience of an individual who does not fit the stereotype. The Macpherson Report (1999) on the murder of Stephen Lawrence recorded that members of the inquiry had heard about racist attitudes amongst young children during the public hearings. It is important to differentiate between examples of prejudice and intolerance and children's natural curiosity: at times children will observe and state differences. There is no malice in such statements and they can be used to appreciate and to value difference. Children draw from their experience of different contexts (the hospital, dentist, child-minder, learning setting, neighbours, friends and television) and generalize their knowledge when meeting individuals from different minority ethnic groups (Puckett and Black, 2001) and other groups. Such experiences can be reinforced or mediated by members of their family and other caregivers. Thus it is important for professionals to model inclusive and accepting attitudes. Prejudice, including racism and classism, have no place in our settings (Charlesworth, 2000). There may be a sense, as Paley (1992) suggests, that our classrooms can be nicer than the outside world and we should strive to ensure that this is the case so that children can develop their attitudes in a supportive environment.

Practical tasks

Plan a learning activity for your children that involves them meeting with an older person from the local community and finding out about their childhood. Ask the adult to bring an old toy or a photograph from when they were younger. Give the adult opportunity to speak briefly about their favourite childhood memories and encourage the children to ask questions.

- How did the children relate to the visitor?
- Did their questions show an appreciation of the memories that were shared, or did they relate more to the children's own interests and experiences?
- How could you develop the activity further to help the children appreciate the experience of others?
- Were the children able to appreciate the concepts of past and present, and how was this demonstrated?

Team work

Working with fellow professionals provides one way to model a sense of community and to support children's learning. By working together we are able to show that it is good to depend on others, to ask for and to receive help and to give thanks and praise to one another. If we are willing to be open and to share our thoughts and feelings with children we can demonstrate the importance of friendship and demonstrate how to say sorry or thank you. Children are very aware of how adults relate and pick up quickly when there are tensions or disagreements; having a sense of our positive professional relationships can help them to feel safe and secure in their learning settings.

Team work also extends to our relationships with parents and carers. The ways in which we make parents/carers welcome and our conversations and communication with them show children that we value their backgrounds and lives beyond the classroom. The diversity of such circumstances has been outlined earlier in the chapter and it is important that we seek to include all those who care for children. If we do not prioritize children's social development it is unlikely that their cognitive development is going to be maximized. Team work with parents/carers, utilizing their knowledge, skills and understanding, can be very beneficial in helping to extend children's experience of the world and in building a sense of community (DfES, 2007).

Parents and carers may be partners in many ways: offering help in the setting; attending meetings and courses; running services such as a home-school association; serving as governors or committee members; and helping to produce and organize resources. For over twenty years legislation and guidance from the government has strongly encouraged working in partnership with parents and carers. The 1988 Education Reform Act emphasized parental choice and schools' accountability to parents and the Children Act of 1989 formalized the concept of parental responsibility. The publication of the Curriculum Guidance for the Foundation Stage (QCA, 2000), Birth to Three Matters (DfES, 2002), and Every Child Matters (DfES, 2004) acknowledged the expertise of parents and carers and the importance of their involvement in achieving the desired outcomes for their children.

The benefits for parents and carers of such involvement include gaining a broader perspective on their child's development, gaining access to professionals so that they can talk about the child's learning and share concerns and gaining a sense that they are helping the professional to know their child even better (Draper and Duffy, 2006). It is important to remember that learning settings will have changed a great deal since parents and carers were, themselves, at school. They may not be familiar with the curriculum or a variety of pedagogical approaches. It is important to help parents and carers to understand the aims, purposes and processes of the setting so that they can appreciate provision. Some parents/carers will have negative feelings from their own education and these may affect how they feel when entering the setting. The introduction of the National Occupational Standards for Work with Parents (LLUK, 2005) provides a way of developing best practice in this area, to develop the skills of practitioners, to increase retention of professionals and to provide focused feedback to staff.

Conclusion

A sense of community is an essential part of what it means to be human. People are, to various degrees and in different ways, gregarious beings who find purpose, fulfilment and identity through relationships with others. Children are a part of communities from before they are born and in their early years become involved in an increasing circle or breadth of communities. Some of these communities will be very small, comprising a primary carer, family and close friends, and others are larger including their peer group, nursery or school, social organizations, religious groups and neighbours, professionals and service providers. Being able to relate to others in positive ways is an essential part of being a part of such communities and gaining a sense of belonging. It also provides the opportunity to experience difference and to gain the confidence necessary to accept and appreciate diversity.

References

Aboud, F. (1988) *Children and Prejudice*. Oxford: Basil Blackwell

Aktar, N. (2002) *Samira's Eid*. London: Mantra

Charlesworth, R. (2000) *Understanding Child Development: for adults who work with young children (5th edition)*. Albany: Delmar

Commission on Integration and Cohesion (2007) *Our Shared Future*. Sine loco: CIC

Cowie, H., Smith, P. K., Boulton, M. and Lover, R. (1994) *Cooperation in the Multi-ethnic Classroom*. London: David Fulton

DCSF (2007) *Guidance on the Duty to Promote Community Cohesion*. Nottingham: Department for Children, Schools and Families

DCSF (2008) *Statutory Framework for the Early Years Foundation Stage.* London: Department for Children, Schools and Families

DfES (2002) *Birth to Three Matters: A Framework to Support Children in the Earliest Years.* London: Department for Education and Skills

DfES (2004) *Every Child Matters: change for children in schools.* London: Department for Education and Skills

DfES (2007) *The Early Years Foundation Stage: Setting the Standard for Learning, Development and Care for Children from Birth to Five; Practice Guidance.* London: Department for Education and Skills

Draper, L. and Duffy, B. (2006) Working with Parents in G. Pugh and B. Duffy (eds) *Contemporary Issues in The Early Years,* 4th Edition. London: Sage Publications

Edwards, C. P. and Lewis, M. (1979) Young Children's Concepts of Social Relations: Social Functions and Social Objects in M. Lewis and L. A. Rosenblum (eds) *The Child and its Family.* New York: Plenum Press

Fabian, H. and Dunlop, A. (2002). *Transitions in the Early Years.* London: Routledge Falmer

Finkelstein, N. W. and Haskins, R. (1983) Kindergarten children prefer same-color peers. *Child Development.* 54, 502–508

Gilmore, R. (1994) *Lights for Gita.* Toronto: Second Story Press

Graham, C. and Hill, M. (2003) *Negotiating the Transition to Secondary School (SCRE Spotlight 89).* Glasgow: University of Glasgow, SCRE Centre

Hest, A. (2001) *The Friday Night's of Nana.* Cambridge: Candlewick Press

Johnstone, K. (2002). The transition to high school: a journey of uncertainty. Paper presented at the *Australian Association for Research in Education Conference,* Brisbane, Queensland, 1–5 December [online]. Available: http://www.aare.edu.au/02pap/joh02562.htm [4 December, 2008]

Linden, J. (1998) *Equal Opportunities in Practice.* London: Hodder and Stoughton

LLUK (2005) *National Occupational Standards for Work with Parents.* London: Lifelong Learning UK.

Macpherson, W. (1999) *The Stephen Lawrence Inquiry: Report of an Inquiry by Sir William Macpherson of Cluny. http://www.archive.official documents.co.uk/document/cm42/4262/4262.htm*

Margetts, K. (2003). Children bring more to school than their backpacks: starting school down under' (Themed Monograph Series), *European Early Childhood Education Research Journal,* 1, 5–14

Morris, J. and Woolley, R. (2008) *The Family Diversities Reading Resource.* Lincoln: Bishop Grosseteste University College

Moyles, J., Adams, S. and Musgrove, A. (2002). *Study of Pedagogical Effectiveness in Early Learning (DfES Research Report 363).* London: DfES

OFSTED (2004) *Transition from the Reception Year to Year 1: an Evaluation by HMI (HMI 2221).* London: Office for Standards in Education

Paley, V. (1992) *You Can't Say You Can't Play.* Cambridge: Cambridge University Press

Papalia, D., Gross, D. and Feldman, R. (2003) *Child Development: A Topical Approach.* New York: McGraw Hill

Pianta R. C., Rimm-Kaufman, S. E. and Cox, M. J. (1999). Introduction: an ecological approach to kindergarten transition in Pianta, R. C. and Cox, M. J. (eds) *The Transition to Kindergarten.* Baltimore,: Paul H Brookes Publishing

Puckett, M. and Black, J. (2001) *The Young Child: Development from Prebirth Through Age Eight* (3rd Edition). Upper Saddle River: Prentice Hall

Pugh, G. and Duffy, B. (2006) *Contemporary Issues in the Early Years,* 4th Edition. London: Sage Publications

QCA (2000) *Curriculum Guidance for the Foundation Stage.* London: Qualifications and Curriculum Authority

Sanders, D., White, G., Burge, B., Sharp, C., Eames, A., McEune, R. and Grayson, H. (2005) *A Study of the Transition from the Foundation Stage to Key Stage 1.* Nottingham: NFER & DfES

Siraj-Blatchford, I., Sylva, K., Muttock, S., Gilden, R. and Bell, D. (2002). *Researching Effective Pedagogy in the Early Years (DfES Research Report 356).* London: DfES

Smith, P., Cowie, H. and Blades, M. (2003) *Understanding Children's Development* (4th Edition). Malden: Blackwell Publishing

Stephen, C. and Cope, P. (2001). *Moving on to Primary 1: An Exploratory Study of the Experience of Transition from Pre-School to Primary (Insight 3).* Edinburgh: Scottish Executive

Tierney, A. (2007) Travellers and Gypsies. Presentation at a conference to launch the Local Authority Inclusion Strategy: *Turning the Tables: Perception and Realities.* North Lincolnshire Council 2nd March 2007

Woolley, R. (2008) Development, well-being and attainment in M. Cole (ed.) *Professional Attributes and Practice: Meeting the Standards for QTS.* London: Routledge

Woolley, R. and Hanson, F. (2008) *Personal Histories: A Celebration of Childhood Memories.* Lincoln: Bishop Grosseteste University College and Boston Borough Council

Conclusion

The series editors and authors hope that you find this book of interest and use to you in your professional work. If you would like to read more about the subject area, we recommend the following reading and websites to you.

Further reading

Bennet, R., Hamill, A. and Pickford, T. (2007) *Progression in Primary ICT.* Oxford: David Fulton Publishers.

Bisset, R. (2005) *Creative Teaching: History in the Primary Classroom.* London: David Fulton Publishers.

Cooper, H. (2004) *Exploring Time and Place through Play: Foundation Stage - Key Stage 1.* David Fulton: London.

de Bóo M (2004) *The Curriculum Partnership: Early Years Handbook* Sheffield: Geography Association.

Fabian, H. and Dunlop, A. (2002) *Transitions in the Early Years.* London: Routledge Falmer.

Fleer, M. (ed.) (2007) *Young Children: Thinking About the Scientific World* early Childhood Australia: Watson, ACT (also available at *www.earlychildhoodaustralia.org.au*

Harrington, V. in Scoffham, S. (1998) *Teaching about Distant Places.* Sheffield: Geographical Association.

Hillman, M. in Scoffham, S. (1998) *Neighbourhood Safety.* Sheffield: Geographical Association.

Hoodless, P. (2008) *Teaching History in Primary Schools. (Achieving QTS).* Exeter: Learning Matters.

Hoodless, P., Bermingham, S., McCreery, E. and Bowen, P. (2003) *Teaching Humanities in Primary Schools. (Achieving QTS).* Exeter: Learning Matters.

Jahoda, G. Development of Scottish children's ideas and attitudes about other countries. *The Journal of Social Psychology,* 1962, 58, 91–108.

Johnson, J. and Nahmad-Williams, L. (2009) *Early Childhood Studies.* Harlow: Pearson Education.

Johnston, J. (2005) *Early Explorations in Science 2nd Edition* Maidenhead: Open University Press.

Martin, F and Owens, P. (2008) *Caring for Our World: A Practical Guide to ESD for Ages 4–8.* Sheffield: Geographical Association.

Price, H. (2008) *The Really Useful book of ICT in the Early Years.* London: Routledge.

Siraj-Blatchford, I. and Whitebread, D. (2003) *Supporting Information and Communications Technology in the Early Years.* Berkshire: Open University Press.

Siraj-Blatchford, I., Sylva, K., Muttock, S., Gilden, R. and Bell, D. (2002) *Researching Effective Pedagogy in the Early Years* (DfES Research Report 356). London: DfES.

Siraj-Blatchford, J., and MacLeod-Brudenell, I. (1999) *Supporting Science, Design and Technology in the Early Years.* Buckingham: Open University Press.

Spencer, C. in Catling, S. and Martin, F. (2004) *Place Attachment, Place Identity and the Development of the Child's Self-identity: Searching the Literature to Develop an Hypothesis.*

Sweet, B. (1996) 'Design and Technology – The Early Years' in Whitebread, D. (ed.) (1996) *Teaching and Learning in the Early Years.* London: Routledge.

Woolley, R. (2008) Development, well-being and attainment in M. Cole (ed.) *Professional Attributes and Practice: Meeting the Standards for QTS.* London: Routledge.

Useful websites

Becta: the government agency leading the national drive to ensure the effective and innovative use of technology throughout learning. http://www.becta.org.uk/

British Association for Early Childhood Education: resources, advice and publications www.early-education.org.uk

Citized: information about developing citizenship education across different phases of the education system www.citized.info

http://www.bbc.co.uk/education/dynamo/history/ BBC educational site with historical activities

http://www.britishpathe.com/ 3500 hours of British film archive which covers news, sport, social history and entertainment from 1896 to 1970

http://www.hitchams.suffolk.sch.uk/foundation/index.htm

http://www.learningcurve.gov.uk/. Learning Curve is a free online resource for teaching and learning history created by The National Archive. Practitioners will find original documents, photographs and film from The National Archives. The site states that it is for Key Stage 2 children onwards, however I have found it a very rich source of pictorial information that can be used with children at all ranges. Its section called 'snap shots' actually detailed single lesson ideas that are suitable for Key Stage 1.

http://www.qcda.gov.uk/1892.aspx QCA website with ideas of how to teach key historical skills to you children.

ICT in the Early Years: a website related to Homerton children's centre. This site gives good ideas for planning and using ICT with young children. http://foundation.e2bn.org/about.html

ICT in the Foundation Year: Sir Robert Hitcham's Primary School – an excellent starting point for ideas.

Multiverse: a website addressing the educational achievement of pupils from diverse backgrounds www.multiverse.ac.uk

Naace: a website dedicated to advancing education through the appropriate use of information and communications technology. http://www.naace.org/

Personal Histories: a celebration of childhood memories. A resource to help schools to promote community cohesion www.bishopg.ac.uk/personalhistories

If you would like to read more about other key areas of the Early Years Foundation Stage, please see the following:

Communication, Language and Literacy, by Callander, N and Nahmad-Williams, N. (London: Continuum, 2010)

Creative Development, by Compton, A., Johnston, J., Nahmad-Williams, L and Taylor, K. (London: Continuum, 2010)

Personal, Social and Emotional Development, by Broadhead, P., Johnston, J., Tobbell, C. and Woolley, R. (London: Continuum, 2010)

Physical Development, by Cooper, L. and Doherty, J. (London: Continuum, 2010)

Problem Solving, Reasoning and Numeracy, by Beckley, P., Compton, A., Johnston, J. and Marland, H. (London: Continuum, 2010)

Index